This book belongs to...

The Walczak Family

AMERICAN CARDINAL READERS

For Catholic Parochial Schools

BOOK THREE

EDITOR OF LOWER GRADE READERS
EDITH M. McLAUGHLIN

Former Critic Teacher, Parker Practice School,
Normal School, Chicago, Ill.

EDITOR OF UPPER GRADE READERS
T. ADRIAN CURTIS, A.B., LL.B.

District Superintendent, formerly Principal, Alexander Hamilton
Junior High School, New York

ASSOCIATE EDITORS

SISTER MARY AMBROSE, O.S.D., A.M.
(Supervisor)
St. Joseph's College and Academy,
Adrian, Michigan

SISTER MARY GERTRUDE, A.M.
Former Supervisor of Parochial High Schools,
Sisters of Charity, Convent Station
New Jersey

SISTER JAMES STANISLAUS
Former Supervisor of Parochial Schools,
Sisters of St. Joseph of Carondolet, St. Louis

ARTHUR H. QUINN, PH.D., LITT.D.
Professor of English, University of
Pennsylvania

TAN Books
Gastonia, North Carolina

Nihil Obstat:
> Arthur J. Scanlan, S.T.D.
> Censor Librorum

Imprimatur:
> ☩ Patrick Cardinal Hayes
> Archbishop of New York

New York, April 21, 1929

American Cardinal Readers were originally published in 1950 and reprinted in 2013 by Neumann Press, an imprint of TAN Books.

Typesetting and minor revisions and corrections in *American Cardinal Readers: Book 3* © 2021 TAN Books

ISBN: 978-0911845-38-9
Kindle ISBN: 978-1-5051-0519-3
ePUB ISBN: 978-1-5051-0811-8

Published in the United States by
TAN Books
PO Box 269
Gastonia, NC 28053
www.TANBooks.com

Printed in the United States of America

CONTENTS

ACKNOWLEDGMENTS

For permission to use copyright material grateful acknowledgment is made: to Appleton & Company for "The Pied Piper" from *Knights Errant* by Sister M. Madeleva, C. S. C., and "Fairies" from *Starshine and Candlelight* by Sister Mary Angelita: to The Book House for Children for "The Babe Moses," "Piccola," "Jamie Watt and His Grandmother's Tea Kettle" and "The Little Toy Land of the Dutch" from *My Bookhouse* by Olive Beauprè Miller; to Milton Bradley Co. for "The Silver Bell" by Mary H. Frary and Charles M. Stebbins from *The Sunken City and Other Stories*, "The Giant Energy and the Fairy Skill" from *Mother Stories* by Maud Lindsay, "The Grateful Indian" by Lawton B. Evans from *Worthwhile Stories*, and "How Primrose Went to the Party" from *Tell Me Another Story* by Carolyn Sherwin Bailey; to The Century Co. for *The Elf and the Dormouse* by Oliver Herford from *St. Nicholas Magazine*, and for "The Sandy Road" from *Jataka Tales* by Ellen C. Babbit; to the Catholic Foreign Mission Society of America, for "San Min's Treasure" from *Field Afar Stories*, Volume I; to F. E. Compton & Company for "The Story of Tiny Tim" from *Compton's Pictured Encyclopedia;* to The Devin-Adair Company for "Eugene, the Youngest" and "St. Dorothy, God-given" from *Children of the Kingdom* by Mary Adelaide Garnett; to Duffield and Company for "The Little Weed" from *Topaz Story Book*, "A Spring Lilt," "The Wind, a Helper" by Mary Stewart, and "The Little Acorn" by Lucy Wheelock, from *Emerald Story Book* by A. M. and E. L. Skinner; to A. Flanagan Company for "What Broke the China Pitcher" from *Cat-Tails and Other Tales* by Mary Howliston; to The Grolier Society for "How the Children Saved the Town," adapted by permission; original copyright by the publishers of *The Book of Knowledge;* to Houghton Mifflin Co. for "Late" from *Poems* by Josephine Preston Peabody; to P. J. Kenedy & Sons for "A Child's Wish" by Rev. Abram J. Ryan; to Lothrop, Lee & Shepard Co. for "Riddles" from *The Joyous Guests* by Maud Lindsay and Emily Poulsson; to Laidlaw Brothers for "The Flag Goes By" by Hay Holcomb Bennet; to Francis A. Litz for "Hide-and-Seek" from *The Poetry of Father Tabb* published by Dodd, Mead & Company; to Carl Moon, author of "The Silver Belt," published in *Child Life;* to Penn Publishing Company for "A Child's Evening Prayer" by May L. Duncan, from *Prose and Poetry for Young People;* to Charles Scribner's Sons, for "The Duel" from *Poems of Eugene Field;* to Geo. L. Shuman & Co. for "The Wonderful World" by William Brighty Rands, to Geo. L. Shuman & Co., and Doubleday, Doran & Co., Inc., for "A Busy Day" by Lucy Diamond from *Our Wonder World;* to Frederick A. Stokes Company for "Indian Children" from *For Days and Days, a Year Round Treasury of Verse for Children* by Annette Wynne (copyright, 1919) and "God Is Good" by Jane Taylor from *Original Poems for Infant Minds and Some Others;* to Nancy Byrd Turner, author of "God's Providence," from *The Mayflower;* to The University Publishing Co. for "Winter Night" by Mary F. Butts from *Live Language Lessons* (Third Book) and "The Snow Man" by W. W. Ellsworth from *Live Language Lessons* (First Book); to Albert Whitman and Company for "Abraham Lincoln's Education" by Mollie C. Winchester from *Oft-Told Tales of Lincoln;* and to The Youth's Companion for "The Calico's Story" and "The Rescue of Old Glory" by Mrs. J. W. Wheeler

GOD'S PROVIDENCE

God gives so many lovely things!
He gives the bird his feathery wings,
The butterfly its colors fair,
The bee a velvet coat to wear.

He gives the garden all its flowers,
And sun to make them grow, and showers;
Red apples for the old bent tree,
Wheat in the meadow blowing free;

Cool grass upon the summer hills,
And silvery streams to turn the mills.
He gives the shining day, and then
The quiet starry night again.

He gives my home—a place to stay,
And laugh, and dream, and work, and play,
The pleasant rooms and windows wide,
And cozy, rosy fireside;

And books to read and folks to love me,
And His good care to watch above me.
It's like a song a person sings—
God gives so many happy things!

THE LITTLE WEED

"You're nothing but a weed," said the children in the fall. The little weed hung its head in sorrow. No one seemed to think that a weed was of any use.

By and by the snow came and the cold winds

blew. There were many hungry little birds hunting for food.

"Twit! Twit! Twee!
See! See! See!"

sang a merry little bird one cold morning.

"Here is a lovely weed full of nice brown seeds!" And he made a good meal from those seeds that morning. Then three other little birds came to share the feast.

The little weed was so happy that she held her head up straight and tall again.

"That is what I was meant for," she said. "I am good for something. Four hungry little birds had as many seeds as they wished for their breakfast. Next year I'll grow as many seeds as I can to feed many more hungry little birds. Good-by, little birds," she called out to the little feathery friends. "Come again next year. I'll have another dinner for you."

"Good-by, little weed," sang the birds. "We thank you for the fine meal we have had. You'll

see us again next year. It is so hard to get
enough to eat during the cold weather. We are
grateful to you for holding your seeds for us."

"It's nice to find that one is of some use after
all, isn't it?" called out the little weed to her
neighbor in the next field.

THE BROWN BIRDS

The brown birds are flying
　Like leaves through the sky,
The flowerets are calling,
　"Dear birdlings, good-by!"

The bird voices falling,
　So soft from the sky,
Are answering the flowerets,
　"Dear playmates, good-by."

5

THE PIED PIPER

Brave Piper October, what tune do you blow
That the leaves are bewitched and wherever
you go
They flutter and follow, agleam and aglow?
From oak tree and bramble, from high tree
and low,
They flock to the sound of the piping they know,
And down from the tall trees of heaven, O ho!
Come dancing and glancing the white leaves
of snow.

THE DARNING NEEDLE

Once there was a darning needle who forgot how coarse and thick she was. She was always telling the fingers, when they held her, to be careful to treat her with respect.

One day the cook used her to sew her old slipper.

"How dare she give me such dirty work to do!" the needle cried to the fingers. "I am much too fine for such work. There! I knew it. I broke."

"Let's drop her on the floor," Mr. Thumb said to his brothers. "She thinks she is so fine that no one will see her."

"No," First Finger said; "the cook is going to fix her." So the fingers held her while the cook put some sealing wax on the broken needle. Then she stuck the darning needle in her dress.

"This is much better," the darning needle said. "I have been raised to a better place in the world."

"You may not stay there very long," Mr. Thumb laughed. "You are much too fine."

Soon his words came true; for, as the cook was washing dishes, the darning needle dropped into the sink.

"Well, well," she said, as she felt herself in the water, "I'm really going on a journey. I knew I was fine. All fine people go on journeys."

Soon the darning needle found herself in the gutter. She was still very proud, even though she had to look up at the things that floated over her.

"Look at that common piece of wood!" she said. "How little of the great world it knows! See that bit of paper! Once it was a page in a book. What is it now?"

The darning needle lay in the gutter for several days. She was not alone, but she thought

8

herself so much above the other things there, that she spoke to no one.

At last, part of a broken bottle was thrown into the gutter. The darning needle thought it was a diamond as it lay sparkling.

"Here, now," she thought, "is some one that I should know. He is not quite so fine as I, but he is not like the other common people that are here."

"Pardon me," she began; "you are a diamond, are you not?"

The glass knew better, but it was just as proud as the darning needle, and wanted people to think well of him.

"Oh, yes," he replied.

"My home was a lady's box," the darning needle said. "The lady had five fingers whose only work in the world was to take me out and put me back into the box."

"Were the fingers of a fine family, too?" asked the glass.

"No," replied the darning needle. "Mr. Thumb was short and fat and rude. He was always laughing at my fine manners. But he didn't know the world. He had been hardly any place outside the kitchen.

"Mr. First Finger was common, too. He pushed me into a coarse slipper one day, but I was too fine, and broke.

"Mr. Middle Finger wasn't much better. He helped Mr. First Finger, and laughed when I broke.

"Mr. Ring Finger was the best one of that family, but that isn't saying much for him.

"Mr. Little Finger was too small to have any manners. But I fear if he lives with his brothers, his manners will be as coarse as theirs."

"You must be thankful that you have left that rude family behind you," replied the piece of glass.

"Indeed, yes," said the darning needle. "That was why I took this journey."

Just then a stream of water came into the gutter, so that the gutter flowed over, and the glass was carried away.

"So he is going away, too," the darning needle said. "I shall stay. I am too fine to go with that crowd. Sometimes I think that the sun is looking for me. Well, I shall not ask him, but if he wants me for a sunbeam, I shall go with him gladly."

One day a boy, who was looking for his marble in the gutter, stuck his finger with the darning needle.

"Well," he said, as he picked up the needle, "what are you doing in the gutter?"

"You are rude, too. How dare you speak to a young lady like that!" the darning needle said; but the boy didn't hear her.

Then the boy saw an egg-shell sailing along down the gutter, and he put the darning needle into the shell.

"This is a pleasant change," the darning needle

11

said. "No fear of being seasick either, for I
have a stomach of steel."

At that moment, a big wagon ran over the
egg-shell.

"What is that?" thought the darning needle.
"Am I seasick? Oh, I am breaking!"

The wagon crushed the egg-shell, but the
darning needle did not break. She was lying
there right on the ground, and she is lying
there still for all I know.*

*From The Reynolds Readers published by Noble and Noble, New York. Used by special
permission.

12

THE WONDERFUL WORLD

Great, wide, beautiful, wonderful World
With the wonderful water around you curled,
And the wonderful grass upon your breast,
World, you are beautifully dressed.

The wonderful air is over me,
And the wonderful wind is shaking the tree—
It walks on the water, and whirls the mills,
And talks to itself on the top of the hills.

You friendly Earth, how far do you go,
With the wheat fields that nod, and the rivers
　　that flow,
With cities and gardens and cliffs and isles,
And people upon you for thousands of miles?

Ah! you are so great, and I am so small,
I hardly can think of you, World, at all;
And yet, when I said my prayers to-day,
My mother kissed me, and said, quite gay,

"If the wonderful World is great to you,
And great to Father and Mother, too,
"You are more than the Earth, though you are
　　such a dot!
You can love and think, and the Earth cannot!"

THE WONDERFUL MESSAGE

There never would have been anything but happiness in this world if Adam and Eve had not disobeyed God. It was this sin of disobedience that closed not only the gates of Paradise but the gates of Heaven as well.

When our first parents saw how angry God was with them, they were sad. Although God was angry, He pitied them and told them that one day He would send a Redeemer to open again the gates of Heaven. He said that this Redeemer would be His own beloved Son.

Years and years passed by and the world had become very wicked. There were many people, however, who remembered God's promise and eagerly awaited the Saviour's coming. Among them was a holy maiden named Mary.

Mary was the daughter of Joachim and Anne, two very holy people. When she was but three years old, her parents took her to the temple. They left her to grow up in this holy place because they wished her to learn to know and love God. Many of the pious Jews of the time sent their little girls to the temple to live and to be educated.

The years spent at the temple were happy ones for Mary. She learned to pray and to read the Sacred Books. She liked best to read the parts that told of God's promise to send His Son to earth.

Mary did not leave the temple until she was fourteen years of age. She was a lovely maiden and never allowed the smallest spot of sin to touch her soul. She was as pure as a lily and loved God with all her heart.

One day, as she knelt praying, an angel shining with light and glory appeared before her. The angels, as you know, are God's messengers, and the message this angel had to carry was the holiest that had ever been sent to earth.

Mary was surprised and startled when the angel bowed low and said, "Hail, full of grace, the Lord is with thee." She was troubled at the angel's greeting and she did not understand his words. When the angel saw this, he at once explained to her the message he had brought. He said, "Fear not, Mary, for you have found favor with God." Then he told her that the time had come for the Redeemer to be born and that God wanted her to be His mother. The Child was to be named Jesus and He would show all people the way to Heaven.

Mary was too humble to believe that she was worthy of so great an honor, but she wanted to do God's will in all things. When the angel finished speaking, she said, "Behold the handmaid of the Lord."

We call the day on which the angel announced to Mary that she was to be the Mother of God, the feast of the Annunciation. Every year on the twenty-fifth of March we celebrate it in a very special way; and every time we say "Hail, Mary, full of grace," we think of the angel's message and what it means to all men.

THE ANNUNCIATION

An angel bright
　From God was sent;
To Mary's home
　His flight he bent.
He found the place
　Wherein she dwelt;
She heard God's message
　As she knelt;
Obedient, she bowed her head,
"I am Thy handmaid, Lord," she said.

THE LITTLE ACORN

It was a little acorn that hung on the bough of a tree.

It had a tender green cup and a beautifully carved saucer to hold it. The mother oak fed it with sap every day, the birds sang good-night songs above it, and the wind rocked it gently to and fro. The oak leaves made a soft green shade above it, so the sun could not shine too warmly on its green cover, and it was as happy as an acorn could be.

There were many other acorns on the tree, and the mother tree, through her wind voices, whispered loving words to all her babies.

The summer days were so bright and pleasant that the acorn never thought of anything but sunshine and an occasional shower to wash the dust off the leaves. But summer ends, and the autumn days came. The green cup of the acorn turned to a brown cup, and it was well that it grew stiffer and harder, for the cold winds began to blow.

The leaves turned from green to golden brown, and some of them were whisked away by the wind. The little acorn began to grow uneasy.

"Isn't life all summer?" it said.

"No," whispered the mother oak; "the cold days come and the leaves must go and the acorns too. I must soon lose my babies."

"Oh! I could never leave this kind bough," said the frightened acorn. "I should be lost and forgotten if I were to fall."

So it tried to cling all the closer to its bough, but at last it was alone there. The leaves were blown away, and some of them had made a blanket for the brown acorns lying on the ground. One night the tree whispered this message to the lonely acorn:

"This tree is only your home for a time. This is not your true life. Your brown shell is only the cover for a living plant, which can never be set free until the hard shell drops away, and that can never happen until you are buried in the ground and wait for the spring to call you into life. So let go, little acorn, and fall to the ground, and some day you will wake to a new and glorious life."

The acorn listened and believed, for was not the tree its sheltering mother? So it bade her farewell, and, losing its hold, dropped to the ground.

Then, indeed, it seemed as if the acorn were lost. That night a high wind blew and covered it deep under a cover of oak leaves. The next day a cold rain washed the leaves closer together, and trickling streams from the hillside swept some earth over them. The little acorn was buried.

"But I shall wake again," it said, and so it fell asleep. It might have been cold; but the frost fairies wove a soft, white snow blanket to cover it, and so it was kept warm.

If you had walked through the woods that winter, you would have said the acorn was gone, but then you could not have seen the life slumbering within the brown cover. But spring came and called to all the sleeping things underground to waken and come forth. The acorn heard and tried to move, but the brown shell held it fast. Some raindrops trickled through the ground to moisten the shell, and one day the pushing life within was set free. The brown shell was of no more use and was lost in the ground, but the young plant was to live. It heard voices calling it upward. It must rise. "A new and glorious life," the mother oak had said.

"I must rise," the acorn said, and up the living plant came, up to the world of sunshine and beauty. It looked around. There was the same green moss in the woods, the same singing brook.

"And I shall live and grow," it said.

"Yes," called the mother oak, "you are now an oak tree. This is your real life."

And the tiny oak was glad and tried to stretch higher toward the sun.

THE ACORN AND THE PUMPKIN

One fine autumn day a young country lad was wandering about in his father's corn field. Growing tired, he threw himself down under an oak tree that grew near by.

Looking up at the branches overhead, he said to himself: "How strange God's ways are. To think of putting tiny acorns on a strong tree like the oak, and fine large pumpkins on vines so slender. I'm sure a great mistake has been made. Had only my opinion been asked when God set out to make the world, I would have put the pumpkin on the oak tree and the acorn on the vine."

Soon after this, he fell asleep. As he slept, an acorn fell plump on his nose. "Oh! oh!" he cried, awakening with a start. "What could that have been?" He spied the tiny acorn. "Well! well!" he exclaimed, "I now know that God understood His work and had good reasons for the things He did. Woe unto me had a pumpkin, instead of an acorn, hit my nose."

A BUSY DAY

Mr. Squirrel is so busy
   On this bright October day;
Soon the winter will be coming,
   So he has no time for play.
Nuts all crisp and brown he gathers;
   "I must put them by," says he,
"Where no little boy can find them,
   In my pantry in the tree."

THE SANDY ROAD

Once upon a time a merchant, with his goods packed in many carts, came to a desert. He was on his way to the country on the other side of the desert.

The sun shone on the fine sand, making it as hot as the top of a stove. No man could walk on it in the sunlight. But at night, after the sun went down, the sand cooled, and then men could travel upon it.

So the merchant waited until after dark, and then set out. Besides the goods that he was going to sell he took jars of water and of rice, and firewood, so that the rice could be cooked.

All night long he and his men rode on and on. One man was the pilot. He rode first for he knew the stars, and by them he guided the drivers.

At daybreak they stopped and camped. They unyoked the oxen, and fed them. They built fires and cooked rice. Then they spread a great awning over all the carts and the oxen, and the men lay down under it to rest until sunset.

In the early evening, they again built fires and cooked rice. After supper, they folded the awning and put it away. They yoked the oxen and as soon as the sand was cool, started again on their journey across the desert.

Night after night they traveled in this way, resting during the heat of the day. At last one morning the pilot said: "In one more night we shall get out of the sand." The men were glad to hear this, for they were tired.

After supper that night the merchant said: "You may as well throw away nearly all the water and the firewood. By to-morrow we shall be in the city. Yoke the oxen and start on."

Then the pilot took his place at the head of the line. But instead of sitting up and guiding the drivers, he lay down in the wagon. Soon he was fast asleep, because he had not slept for many nights, and the light had been so strong in the daytime that he had not slept well then.

All night long the oxen went on. Near daybreak, the pilot awoke and looked at the last stars fading in the light. "Halt!" he cried to the drivers. "We are in the same place where we were yesterday. The oxen must have turned around while I slept."

They unyoked the oxen, but there was no water for them to drink. They had thrown away the water that was left the night before. So the men spread the awning over the carts, and the oxen lay down tired and thirsty. The men, too, lay down saying, "The wood and water are gone —we are lost."

But the merchant said to himself, "This is no time for me to sleep. I must find water. The oxen cannot go on if they do not have water to drink. The men must have water. They cannot cook the rice unless they have water. If I give up, we all shall be lost."

On and on he walked, keeping close watch of the ground. At last he saw a tuft of grass. "There must be water somewhere below, or that grass would not be there," he said.

He ran back, shouting to the men, "Bring the spade and the hammer!"

They jumped up and ran with him to the spot where the grass grew. They began to dig and by and by they struck a rock and could dig no farther. Then the merchant jumped down into

31

the hole they had dug, and put his ear to the rock. "I hear water running under this rock," he called to them. "We must not give up!" Then the merchant came up out of the hole and said to the serving lad: "My boy, if *you* give up we are lost! You go down and try!"

The boy stood up straight and raised the hammer high above his head and hit the rock as hard as ever he could. He would not give in. They must be saved. Down came the hammer. This time the rock broke. The boy had hardly time to get out of the well before it was full of water. The men drank as if they could never get enough, and then they watered the oxen.

Then they split up their extra yokes and axles and built a fire, and cooked their rice. Feeling better, they rested through the day. They set up a flag on the well for travelers to see.

At sundown, they started on again, and the next morning reached the city, where they sold the goods, and then returned home.

THE GIANT ENERGY AND THE FAIRY SKILL

THE GIANT ENERGY

Long, long ago, when there were giants to be seen, as they might be seen now if we only looked in the right place, there lived a young giant who was very strong and very willing, but found it hard to get work to do.

The name of this giant was Energy, and he was so great and clumsy that people were afraid to trust their work to him.

If he were asked to put a bell in the church steeple, he would knock the steeple down, before he finished the work. If he were sent to reach a broken weather vane, he would tear off part of the roof in his zeal. So, at last, people would not employ him and he went away to the mountains to sleep; but he could not rest, even though other giants were sleeping as still as great rocks under the shade of the trees.

Young Giant Energy could not sleep, for he was too anxious to help in the world's work; and he went down into the valley, and begged so piteously for something to do that a good woman gave him a basket of china to carry home for her.

"This is child's play for me," said the giant as he set the basket down at the woman's house,

but he set it down so hard that every bit of the china was broken.

"I wish a child had brought it for me," answered the woman, and the young giant went away sorrowful. He climbed the mountain and lay down to rest; but he could not stay there and do nothing, so he went back to the valley to look for work.

There he met the good woman. She had forgiven him for breaking her china, and had made up her mind to trust him again; so she gave him a pitcher of milk to carry home.

"Be quick in bringing it," she said, "lest it sour on the way."

The giant took the pitcher and made haste to run to the house; and he ran so fast that the milk was spilled and not a drop was left when he reached the good woman's house.

The good woman was sorry to see this, although she did not scold; and the giant went back to his mountain with a heavy heart.

35

Soon, however, he was back again, asking at every house:

"Isn't there something for me to do?" and again he met the good woman, who was here, there and everywhere, carrying soup to the sick and food to the hungry.

When she met the young Giant Energy, her heart was full of love for him; and she told him to make haste to her house and fill her tubs with water, for the next day was wash day.

Then the giant made haste with mighty strides towards the good woman's house, where he found her great tubs; and, lifting them with ease, he carried them to the cistern and began to pump.

He pumped with such force and with so much delight, that the tubs were soon so full that they ran over, and when the good woman came home she found her yard as well as her tubs full of water.

The young giant had such a downcast look, that the good woman could not be angry with him; she only felt sorry for him.

The Kind Old Woman Tells Giant Energy About Fairy Skill

"Go to the Fairy Skill, and learn," said the good woman, as she sat on the doorstep. "She will teach you, and you will be a help in the world after all."

"Oh! how can I go?" cried the giant, giving a jump that sent him up over the tree tops, where he could see the little birds in their nests.

"Don't go so fast," said the good woman. "Stand still and listen! Go through the meadow, and count a hundred daffodils; then turn to your right, and walk until you find a mullein stalk that is bent. Notice the way it bends, and walk in that direction till you see a willow tree. Behind this willow tree runs a little stream. Cross the water by the way of the shining pebbles, and when you hear a strange bird singing you can see the fairy palace and the workroom where the Fairy Skill teaches her school. Go to her with my love and she will receive you."

GIANT ENERGY FINDS FAIRY SKILL AND LEARNS TO BE A HELPER

The young giant thanked the good woman, stepped over the meadow fence, and counted the

daffodils, "One, two, three," until he had counted
a hundred. Then he turned to the right, and
walked through the long grass to the bent
mullein stalk, which pointed to the right; and
after he had found the brook and crossed by way
of the shining pebbles, he heard a strange bird
singing, and saw among the trees the fairy palace.

He never could tell how it looked; but he
thought it was made of sunshine, with the

glimmer of green leaves reflected on it, and that it had the blue sky for a roof.

That was the palace; and at one side of it was the workshop, built of strong pines and oaks; and the giant heard the hum of wheels, and the noise of fairy looms, where the fairies wove carpets of fairy rainbow threads.

When the giant came to the door, the doorway stretched itself for him to pass through. He found Fairy Skill standing in the midst of the workers; and when he had given her the good woman's love, she received him kindly. Then she set him to work, bidding him sort a heap of tangled threads that lay in a corner like a great bunch of bright-colored flowers.

This was hard work for the giant's clumsy fingers, but he was very patient about it. The threads would break, and he got some of them into knots; but when Fairy Skill saw his work, she said:

"Very good for to-day."

Then touching the threads with her wand, she changed them into a tangled heap again. The next day the giant tried again, and after that again, until every thread lay unbroken and untangled.

Then Fairy Skill said, "Well done," and led him to a loom and showed him how to weave.

This was harder work than the other had been; but Giant Energy was patient, although

41

many times before his strip of carpet was woven the fairy touched it with her wand, and he had to begin over.

At last it was finished, and the giant thought it was the most beautiful carpet in the world.

Fairy Skill took him next to the potter's wheel, where cups and saucers were made out of clay; and the giant learned to be steady, to shape the

cup as the wheel whirled round, and to take heed of his thumb, lest it slip.

The cups and saucers that were broken before he could make beautiful ones would have been enough to set the queen's tea table!

Fairy Skill then took him to the goldsmith, and there he was taught to make chains and bracelets and necklaces; and after he had learned all these things, the fairy told him that she had three trials for him. Three pieces of work he must do; and if he did them well, he could go again into the world, for he would then be ready to be a helper there.

"The first task is to make a carpet," said Fairy Skill, "a carpet fit for a palace floor."

Giant Energy sprang to his loom, and made his silver shuttle glance under and over, under and over, weaving a most beautiful pattern.

As he wove, he thought of the way by which he had come; and his carpet became as green as the meadow grass, and lovely daffodils grew on

it. When it was finished, it was almost as beautiful as a meadow full of flowers!

Then the fairy said that he must turn a cup fine enough for a king. The giant made a cup in the shape of a flower; and when it was finished, he painted birds upon it with wings of gold. When she saw it, the fairy cried out with delight.

"One more trial before you go," she said. "Make me a chain that a queen might be glad to wear."

So Giant Energy worked by day and by night and made a chain of golden links; and in every link was a pearl as white as the shining pebbles in the brook. A queen might well have been proud to wear this chain.

After he had finished, Fairy Skill kissed him, and sent him away to be a helper in the world. She gave him the things which he had made, so that he might give them to the one he loved best.

The young giant crossed the brook, passed the willow, found the mullein stalk, and counted the daffodils.

When he had counted a hundred, he stepped over the meadow fence and came to the good woman's house.

The good woman was at home, so he went in at the door and spread the carpet on the floor, and the floor looked like the floor of a palace.

He set the cup on the table, and the table looked like the table of a king; and he hung the chain around the good woman's neck, and she was more beautiful than a queen.

And this is the way that young Giant Energy learned to be a helper in the world.

THE BABE MOSES

There rose a King over Egypt who knew nothing of God. Therefore he thought no good in his heart. And he said: "There live in the midst of our land the Children of Israel. They are not of our people; yet they are more in numbers than we. I fear lest they have too many babes that grow up to be strong men and stand against us. Come, then; let us throw into the river every boy babe that is born unto them."

Now there was at this time in Egypt a certain man and his wife of the Children of Israel, and there was born unto them a boy babe, even such a one as Pharaoh the King had commanded should be thrown into the river. But he was a goodly child, and his mother loved him and held him close to her heart and cherished him.

46

And she kept him hid three months that Pharaoh's servants might not find him and throw him into the river.

And when she could no longer hide him, she gathered bulrushes from the river bank and made of them a little ark. And she daubed the ark with mud and pitch and put her babe therein, and laid him in the rushes by the river.

Then she bade his sister stand afar off and watch what would be done to him. And she kissed the little one and went back to her home; for her trust was in God, and she knew that God was with the child to save him.

And it came to pass that the daughter of Pharaoh the King came down to wash herself at the river; and her maidens walked along by the river's side.

When she saw the ark among the rushes, she sent her maid to get it. And when she had laid back the coverings, she saw the little babe, and behold! he was crying.

Then Pharaoh's daughter was filled with pity for the child, and she took him to her and said,

"This is a babe of the Children of Israel, even such a one as my father has commanded should be thrown into the river."

But, as she held the little one in her arms and saw how he wept, God touched her heart, and she thought within herself to save the child, for she knew that the King, her father, would grant unto her whatsoever she asked of him. So she cried out to her maids and said, "I will ask of the King, my father, that I may keep this little one. He shall be as my own son."

Then came the sister of the babe, who had been watching, and said to Pharaoh's daughter, "Shall I go and call unto thee a nurse of the women of Israel that she may care for the child for thee?"

And Pharaoh's daughter said to her, "Go."

And the maid went and called the child's own mother.

And Pharaoh's daughter said unto the child's mother, "Take this child away and nurse him for me, and I will give thee thy wages."

And the mother took her little babe, and held him close, and rejoiced and gave thanks in her heart that God had saved him.

And she nursed the child and he grew, and when he was no more a babe, she brought him unto Pharaoh's daughter in the house of the King, and Pharaoh's daughter kept him as her own son.

And she called his name, Moses. "Because," she said, "I drew him out of the water."*

*Taken from *My Bookhouse*, edited by Olive Beauprè Miller, with the permission of the publishers, The Book House for Children.

THE CHRIST CHILD IN THE TEMPLE

When Jesus was a little babe, Mary and Joseph had to flee with Him into Egypt because King Herod wanted to put Him to death.

Egypt was a strange land but they stayed there willingly for it was God's will.

After a time an angel appeared to Joseph and said:

"Herod is dead. Take the Child and His Mother and return to your own country."

Joseph told Mary what the angel had said. With hearts full of joy, they at once set out on their homeward journey and went to the little village of Nazareth. Here they lived for many years among their friends and relatives.

Jesus grew tall and strong. He helped His Mother with the work about the house and when He was older, He helped Joseph in the carpenter shop. It was indeed a Holy Family, for they loved God with all their hearts.

Every year, as was the custom of the Jews, Mary and Joseph went up to the temple in Jerusalem to keep the Feast of the Passover. When Jesus was twelve years old, He went with them for the first time. It was a week of much praying and great joy. The city was so crowded with those who came from far and near that many had to sleep in tents along the roadsides.

When the Feast was over, Mary and Joseph, with the other people from Nazareth, started for home. The men walked in one group, the women in another. The children went with either father or mother. All throughout the day Mary thought Jesus was with Joseph, and Joseph thought He was with His Mother. When night came, the Boy was nowhere to be found. No one had seen Him.

Mary and Joseph were frightened. Where could Jesus be? They forgot they were tired and

hungry and at once turned back to look for Him.
When they reached Jerusalem, they went up one
street and down another, always asking the same
question and always getting the same answer:

"We have not seen the Boy."

Weary and footsore, after searching for three days and nights, Mary and Joseph at last came to the temple, where they found Jesus. He was in the midst of the learned doctors and priests, listening to them and asking them questions. All who heard Him were astonished at His wisdom.

How happy Jesus must have been when He turned and saw Mary and Joseph! He must have missed them, for He loved them more than any one on earth.

Mary said to Him:

"Son, why have You done so to us? Behold, Your father and I have sought You sorrowing."

Jesus answered, saying:

"Why is it that you sought Me? Did you not know that I must be about My Father's business?"

The Holy Family now left the temple. The Bible tells us:

"And He went down with them and came to

Nazareth and was subject to them. And His
Mother kept all these words in her heart. And
Jesus advanced in wisdom and age and grace
with God and men."

HIDE-AND-SEEK

You hid your little self, dear Lord,
　　As other children do;
But oh, how great was their reward
　　Who sought three days for You!

THE FROZEN HANDS

I. Ivan's Plan

The Princess Gerda and her little brother were playing in their nursery one afternoon in the winter-time, when the snow lay on the ground and icicles hung from every tree, and the wind was so bitterly cold that the children were not allowed to go out.

"Oh, look, Ivan," cried the little Princess, as she looked out of the window into the castle yard. "See the poor children!"

"Our father will see that they are given money," said Ivan; "he has ordered the servants never to turn any one away from the door."

"I wish we could go down and speak to them," said Gerda. "We never do anything for the poor, and yet our grandmother belonged to the same

family as Queen Elizabeth of Hungary, who was so good to the poor that she worked miracles."

"Well," returned the Prince, "I have a plan in my head, and if you will promise not to tell it to nurse, as you generally do, I will tell you."

"Oh, Ivan, I promise faithfully, and I never told any of your secrets when you made me promise not to."

"Come into the corner, then," said Ivan, drawing into a corner of the big nursery. "Did you listen to Father Nickanor preaching last Sunday, and did you hear what he said about helping those in need? Well, we too must do something for the poor this winter."

"But what shall we do? We are never allowed to go out alone."

"We shall go out on Christmas Eve, when everybody is in church, and Caterina has left us here alone. You must sew some clothes by that time, instead of always making clothes for your dolls, and we must get the cook to give us some food. We can give all the money Grandmother has given us on our birthdays, too."

"Yes," agreed Gerda cheerfully, although she disliked sewing very much. "But, oh, Ivan, have you thought how dark it will be, and the wolves? I heard one howling last Christmas night, when I was in bed."

"Well, of course, if you are going to be afraid,

I must go by myself," answered Ivan, rather crossly. "You are always talking about the poor, so I thought you would be brave enough for that."

"Yes, I will go, Ivan dear," said the little girl, putting her arms around her brother's neck, "and I will begin the sewing to-morrow."

II. Christmas Eve

Every day the little Princess sat sewing for the poor children when she and Ivan were not at lessons or out walking in the grounds with Caterina or sleighing.

Towards Christmas Eve their father and mother went to spend Christmas at the Court of the Czar. You know, they belonged to the Czar's Court, so they had to go each year for the big celebration that was held.

Ivan and Gerda were quite free to carry out their little plans, as Caterina did not trouble

very much about them when the Princess Mother
was away.

On Christmas Eve, when they were sure every
one was in church at confession, they dressed
themselves in their warm furs.

Then they filled a large basket with the
clothes the Princess Gerda had made and
with the good things they had coaxed
from the cook. When all was ready, they

carried the basket downstairs, opened the door and looked out.

It was a bitterly cold night, and the snow lay deep on the ground. The moon was bright and many beautiful stars filled the sky.

"Oh!" shivered Gerda, as they stepped out into the cold.

"Now, then," said Ivan, "are you going to be a baby?"

"No," answered Gerda, but her voice shook.

The moon lighted up the snow until it shone with dazzling brightness, but the shadows cast by the trees and bushes were very dark. What awful thing, thought the little Princess, might not be hidden in the darkness, ready to spring out and pounce upon them as they passed.

"Come on," said the Prince, as they passed by a little cluster of fir trees, "let us hasten, or perhaps Caterina will notice that we are gone, and will come after us."

To tell the truth, he was beginning to be rather

afraid himself, but he was ashamed to have his sister know that.

"We can't go any faster with this heavy basket," gasped Gerda. "Change hands with me, Ivan." Her poor little hands were fast becoming numbed.

They trudged on for about a mile, and then found themselves on the top of a hill, at the foot of which was the village. They could hear the Christmas bells and see the lights of the torches which the people going to church carried in their hands.

"There," said Ivan joyfully, as they put down the basket to rest for a moment; "we have gone more than half the way."

But it was very difficult going down the hill with the heavy basket. It was so slippery that every now and then they slid down a few steps, which ended in a fall. Gerda lost one of her snow-shoes, and Ivan bruised his head very badly in a fall.

"Shall we ever get there?" sobbed Gerda, her little shoeless foot hurting her dreadfully with the cold. "My hands and my foot are freezing, Ivan, and they will drop off."

"So are mine," answered Ivan. "What shall we do if our hands freeze to the basket?"

Gerda sobbed louder than ever, and even Ivan's tears flowed. They were so cold and tired that their courage disappeared.

"Let us pray to the Infant Jesus," said Gerda. "He will not let us freeze so, when we came out on purpose to please Him."

They knelt down and prayed together:

"Jesus, sweetest Infant, born in a stable, laid in a manger, crucified on the hard wood of the cross, help us in our hour of need." It was a little prayer their mother had taught them, and Gerda added to it:

"And please keep our hands from freezing to the basket, dear Jesus."

64

Then they took up their basket, but it seemed to have grown so light that they cried out in wonder.

"You have let some of the things drop out," said Ivan.

"No; it is just as full up to the brim as when we started; and, see, the things are in the same place," said Gerda, lifting a corner of the wolf-skin with which they had covered their treasures. "And, oh!" she cried, "I am quite warm, and the snow feels like a warm bear-skin to my foot, and my hands are like toast."

"So are mine," exclaimed Ivan joyfully. "It is Jesus, Who has answered our prayers. So let us kneel and thank Him from the bottom of our hearts."

They knelt on the snow, which now felt warm to them, and thanked God for helping them.

As they went on down the hill, the snow still felt warm to their feet, and the basket light to carry.

In the first cottage they entered, they found an old woman in bed. She was so very, very old that she shivered with the cold, though there was a large fire burning on the hearth. They covered her with a warm blanket which Gerda had knitted, and she immediately cried out that she no longer felt the cold, and her teeth stopped chattering, and her stiffened fingers grew warm so that she could move them.

The two children passed on through the village giving something from the basket to all the needy ones. There was no one in want who did not receive the very thing he needed most.

At last they came to a hut in which they found a little lame boy. He had not been able to walk, or even move about, for nine years. Gerda gave him the best and nicest things from the cook's store and, putting her little arms around his neck, she kissed him. Immediately the little lame boy felt the pain in his back vanish. He got up and ran to meet his mother, who had just

returned from Mass and Communion, and had
been praying to the Infant Jesus for her little
son.

After a long time, the two children were missed
from the castle. Caterina guessed they must
have gone out into the streets, for she found
their little coats and hats were missing. With the
other servants she started out to look for them.
When she at last found them, at the other end

of the village, she was too relieved to scold, so the two little ones were bundled into the big sleigh and driven home. There had been time, however, for the little runaways to make sad hearts glad.

To this day, in that small village, the fathers and mothers tell their children on Christmas Eve the story of the little Prince and Princess who set out on that day with a large basket of food and clothing in honor of the Infant Jesus. And they never forget to tell how the dear Jesus helped the little ones when their poor little hands were freezing and how He rewarded their devotion by the miraculous cure of the lame boy.

A CHILD'S EVENING PRAYER

Jesus, tender shepherd, hear me!
  Bless Thy little child to-night;
Through the darkness be Thou near me;
  Keep me safe till morning light.

69

All the day Thy hand has led me,
  And I thank Thee for Thy care;
Thou hast warmed and clothed and fed me;
  Listen to my evening prayer.

Keep me now from every danger;
  Let Thine angel guard my bed;
Thou hadst nothing but a manger
  Where to lay Thine infant head.

Let my sins be all forgiven;
  Bless the friends I love so well;
Take me, when I die, to Heaven,
  Happy there with Thee to dwell.

Now I close my eyes so weary,
  Fold my arms upon my breast,
Praying Thee, my God, to bless me,
  As I gently sink to rest.

THE GRATEFUL INDIAN

One summer morning in a New England village Mrs. Grafton was sitting on her porch shelling peas for dinner. John and Jean, her children, were playing around the yard, when an Indian woman, carrying a baby on her back, passed the house. John ran out of the gate and after the woman. He saw something was the

71

matter with the baby, and asked what it was.

"Papoose sick," said the Indian mother, "see doctor."

John said: "Bring the baby in here and my mother will make it well."

The Indian woman followed John into the yard, and Mrs. Grafton took the sick little papoose on her lap and gave it some medicine. After a while the little baby stopped crying and went to sleep in Mrs. Grafton's lap. The Indian mother took her papoose home, saying that Mrs. Grafton was "a good doctor."

The next day the mother again appeared with the baby, and Mrs. Grafton washed it, put some clean clothes on it and gave it some more medicine. After a while the Indian baby got well, and the Indian woman came no more.

That winter was very hard and cold; snow everywhere and cold biting winds. Thanksgiving came, and Mrs. Grafton started to make pies for dinner. She cut up the pumpkin and then looked in the molasses jug. Not a drop of molasses there.

"Oh, my! what shall we do? There is no molasses to make the pies," she exclaimed in dismay. John looked thoughtful.

"I will go and get some from the store," he said, and was off in a moment with the empty jug, right through the woods. The jug was heavy and it was already late in the afternoon, but they must have pies for the next day.

John reached the store. The jug was filled and he started home again. It began to snow as John entered the woods. The path was soon covered and poor John took the wrong turn, then tried to come back, and soon was hopelessly lost. He ran on as fast as he could and then stopped and began to cry. A tall man stood before him. It was an Indian with a gun. John said:

"Please, I am lost. Take me back home." But the Indian took him on his shoulder and

carried him to a camp fire near a tent. There
was an Indian woman with a papoose there.
She looked at John and said a few words to the
tall man who had brought him in. The Indian
grunted and smiled, and then lifted John to his
shoulders, and with him and his jug tramped
through the snow-drifts back to John's home.
He set him down on the doorstep and said:

"My squaw and my papoose you helped last
summer. Me have thanksgiving here," and he
touched his breast and disappeared.

INDIAN CHILDREN

Where we walk to school each day,
Indian children used to play—
All about our native land,
Where the shops and houses stand.

And the trees were very tall,
And there were no streets at all,
Not a church and not a steeple—
Only woods and Indian people.

Only wigwams on the ground,
And at night bears prowling round—
What a different place to-day
Where we live and work and play!

EUGENE, THE YOUNGEST

The room was full of warmth and light, and before the cheery fire on the hearth, a mother and her boys were gathered. Eugene, the youngest, was resting his head on his mother's knee; another boy stood behind her, one hand on her shoulder; a third was writing at a table that was near, and the others were listening eagerly to something the mother was saying. An instant later the boy who was writing dropped his quill and joined the group.

"My little one," the mother repeated, one hand softly patting Eugene's tumbled curls, "tell me, what would you do if the Emperor should order you to bow to the idol he adores?"

The boy sprang to his feet, his eyes glowing. "I would rather die than give up God," he cried. "But, my Mother," he continued, "why does not the Emperor leave us alone? What are we doing to harm him? We obey his laws, all save this one."

"Ah, but that is just the point, little brother," one of the older boys broke in. "He claims that his gods will not answer when he prays to them because we are Christians, and are allowed to live. The time may come soon, Eugene, when you will have to carry out the promise you have just made. May God give us all strength in that day," he added reverently.

There was a heavy rap at the door, and in answer to the "Salve," or "Welcome," of the Romans, a captain of the guard entered the room.

"The Emperor calls for you," he said, "come."

The mother bowed her head. "We will go with you," she replied. There was no sign of fear in her eyes, and as little Eugene placed his hand confidingly in hers, he drew her down to whisper, "I will keep my promise, Mother."

Guarded by the soldiers, the mother and her seven noble boys made their way to the court room. A crowd had gathered to witness the trial, but the boys showed no excitement. One after the other they were asked, "Will you bow to the idols?" One after the other they gave the brave answer, "Never, for Christ is our King."

When the question came to Eugene, the Emperor stopped him. "Think, boy," he urged, "think what it means to say no. You will be

put to death in great pain, and every one will
think of you as a traitor.   But if you bow only
for an instant at the altar of Mars, all will
praise you as a loyal Roman.   Think of this
before you answer."

The boy threw back his head and smiled into
his mother's eyes.   "I would rather die than
give up God," he said.

The Emperor's face grew stern. "You have chosen death; you shall have your will," he cried.

One by one, the boys gave their lives to God, while their suffering mother looked on. Then she stepped forward and willingly followed her sons in giving her life to the Master Whom she had taught them to love.

GOD IS GOOD

God is so good that He will hear,
   Whenever children humbly pray;
He always lends a gracious ear
   To what the youngest child may say.

His own most Holy Book declares
   He loves good little children still;
And that He listens to their prayers,
   Just as a tender Father will.

WHAT BROKE THE CHINA PITCHER

It was a winter night—still, bright, and cold. The wagon wheels and footsteps creaked loudly as they ground into the crisp snow, and even the great, solemn moon looked frosty and cold.

Katrina stood by the sitting room window, looking out.

"It is going to be a dreadful night," said

Father, stirring the fire, "it is growing colder every minute."

"Is it?" said Mother. "Then, Katrina, you must run upstairs and empty the china pitcher in the spare room."

"Yes," said Katrina, but she did not go, for she was looking out at the moonlight, and Mother was rocking baby to sleep.

Fifteen minutes passed. Baby was going to "By-low Land" fast, and Mother spoke again:

"Come, Katrina, go and see to the pitcher. It was Grandma's Christmas present, and we shouldn't like to have it broken."

"Yes, Mother," said Katrina, "I will go in a minute."

"Well, dear, be sure to remember," said Mother and she went off to put baby into her crib. At that moment in came Jamie with a pair of shining new skates, and Katrina forgot all about the pitcher as soon as she saw them.

Just outside the window stood the Cold, listening and watching; and now he chuckled and snapped his icy fingers.

"That little girl will never empty the pitcher," he said to himself. "She's one of the careless kind. Oh, I know them. Let me see—the spare room—that's for company. I'll go spend the night in it. Where is it, I wonder? I will hunt it up."

He knew better than to try to get into the cozy sitting room, with its bright fire, so he slipped softly around the house and peeped in through the kitchen window. Inside was a large stove glowing with coal, and a tea kettle sending out of a cloud of steam.

He shook his head and muttered: "That is no place for me; the heat in there would kill me in a minute; I must look farther."

He went on, peeping in one window after another, until he saw a room with no fire. "Ah," he whispered, "this must be the place. Yes, that is the very pitcher I am going to break; and, if here isn't a fine crack to let me in!" So in he went.

"It is a pretty room," he said, "and it seems a pity to spoil such a handsome pitcher; but Katrina should not have left the water in it."

He stole noiselessly along, chilling everything he touched, until he reached the wash stand. Up the stand he went, nearer and nearer to the pitcher, until he could look into it. "Not much water," he whispered, "but I can make it do," and he spread his icy fingers over it.

The water shivered and drew back, but the icy fingers pressed harder. "Oh," cried the water, "I am so cold!" and it shrank more and more.

Very soon it called out, "If you don't go away, Cold, I shall certainly freeze!"

"Good!" laughed the Cold, "that is just what I want you to do."

All at once the air was filled with many little voices that seemed to come from the pitcher— sharp and clear like little tinkling sleighbells in Fairyland.

"Hurrah!" they cried; "the Cold is making us into beautiful crystals. Oh, won't it be jolly, jolly!"

At that, the Cold pushed his finger straight into the water and it began to freeze. Then such a wonderful thing happened. The drops began arranging themselves in rows and lines that everywhere crossed each other; but they pushed so hard that the pitcher cried out:

"Please stop pushing me so hard; I am afraid I shall break."

"We can't stop," said the drops. "We are freezing, and we must have more room," and they kept on spreading and arranging themselves.

The poor pitcher groaned and called again: "Don't, don't. I can't stand it." But it did no good. The drops kept on saying, "We must have more room." And they pushed steadily and so hard that, at last, with a loud cry, the poor pitcher cracked.

The Cold looked around to see if there was any more mischief he could do. When he found there was none, he stole softly away through the crack in the window.

Just outside was Jack Frost, looking for a good place to hang his pictures. The Cold told him about the pitcher, and they went together, laughing as if it were a good joke.

Upstairs in her snug little bed, Katrina lay, and dreamed that Grandma's pitcher was dancing on the counterpane, in brother Jamie's new skates.

WINTER NIGHT

Blow, wind, blow!
Drift the flying snow!
Send it twirling, whirling overhead!
There's a bedroom in a tree,
Where, snug as snug can be,
The squirrel nests in his cosy bed.

Shriek, wind, shriek!
Make the branches creak!
Battle with the boughs till break of day!
In a snow-cave warm and tight,
Through the icy winter night
The rabbit sleeps the peaceful hours away.

Call, wind, call!
In entry and in hall,
Straight from off the mountain white and wild!
Soft purrs the pussy cat,
On her little fluffy mat,
And beside her nestles close her furry child.

Scold, wind, scold!
So bitter and so bold!
Shake the windows with your tap, tap, tap!
With half-shut, dreamy eyes,
The drowsy baby lies
Cuddled closely in his mother's lap.*

*By Mary F. Butts from *Live Language Lessons*, Third Book. Published by The University Publishing Co.

PICCOLA

Gay was little Piccola! Busy was little Piccola!
Her father was often away from home fishing
far out at sea. Then she and her mother were
left all alone in their little stone cottage, in a
small village in France.

Piccola helped keep the cottage clean; she
scoured the pots and pans; she tended the

geraniums that bloomed in the windows; she dragged in great armfuls of wood for the fire.

"My little Piccola is as busy as the bee," said her mother.

"My little Piccola is as gay as the lark," said her father.

When her work was done, Piccola raced with the other children through the narrow streets of the village, her little wooden shoes going rat-a-tat-too on the cobble-stones, or she climbed up high on the rocks that rose behind the town and looked far out to sea where the sailboats danced in the breeze.

"A jolly good comrade is Piccola," her little playmates said.

But one year, when the yellowed leaves fell from the trees, and the snow began to fall, there came to Piccola's home a time of sadness. Poor had the fishing season been the summer before, and the good father had laid little money by to meet their needs for the winter. He came in from the stormy sea, to go out no more till the spring returned, and he could get no work to earn money through the winter.

"I do not know how we shall ever get on until spring," he mourned

But Piccola was none the less happy.

"God gives us our daily bread," she said, and her little heart was grateful for each day's simple food.

As the weeks slipped by, and their little store of money grew smaller and smaller, the Christmas-tide drew near.

"What shall we do for Piccola?" said the mother, "we are so poor, we cannot buy her even one small gift."

"No," said her father, "not even one small gift."

PICCOLA'S CHRISTMAS

Now close by the church, past which Piccola often romped in her play, there stood a mass of old gray stone, carved with quaint figures that told of the life of Jesus. Stiff and queerly fashioned were the figures, but they had been carved by those who loved the story, and Piccola loved it too. As she carefully traced out all the tale, she said to herself with a heart full of reverence:

"It was Jesus who taught men to know the good God as their father, to let His Goodness shine in their hearts, and to love one another."

So when the Christ-mass drew near and men made ready to celebrate the coming of Jesus Christ to men, Piccola had no thought but that all the earth must rejoice.

"I love the good Christmas-tide!" she cried.

"But, Piccola," said her mother, "do you not know that no gifts can come to you this year?"

"Good gifts must come to all with Christmas," the child made answer, simply.

"Poor little one," said the mother in a low voice to the father, "if we only had one sou to spare to buy her the least little gift."

So the father and mother were sorrowful, but Piccola was happy.

On the night before Christmas, Piccola sang as she swept up the hearth, and when her share of the evening's work was done, she seized her father and mother each by the hand.

"Let us go out and be merry!" she cried.

So they left their dingy little cottage and went out into the village. All the windows were ablaze with lights, and hung with festoons and gay Christmas baubles. So close to the street were the little stone houses, that Piccola and her mother and father could see all the happiness and cheer within.

"Every house but ours is gay," said the father. But Piccola did not even hear him. She was laughing with joy at the joy she saw. Every gay festoon, every gay Christmas bauble, all the happiness and cheer in every house they passed was hers to enjoy! She was richer far than those who had only one cottage with festooned windows!

So they went on to the very last house in the village. There they saw three little children carefully setting their wooden shoes by the fireplace, to be filled with Christmas gifts.

"To-morrow they will be full of goodies!"

"And full of toys!" rang their shrill little voices.

"I shall set out my shoe too!" cried Piccola with shining eyes.

"Piccola, there can be no Christmas gifts for you!" her mother repeated half sobbing. But still Piccola did not hear. Too firm was her faith that every child shared alike in the love of the good God, and none could be shut out from receiving His good gifts.

By the dim candle light she made ready for bed. In her heart was all the joy of the merriment she had seen in the village. Last of all she set by the hearth, where the fire was dying down, her little wooden shoe.

"Through all the year, I have been as good as I know how," she cried, "so I shall find something good here to-morrow."

Then Piccola crept happily into bed, but her mother and father sat long by the embers, and looked sorrowfully at the waiting shoe they had no gifts to fill.

Slowly the night wore away and the gray dawn came. Piccola opened her eyes.

"Christmas is come!" she cried and sprang from her bed. Eagerly, expectantly, she crept to her little shoe.

Her mother and father heard her, and listened with bated breath. "Another minute," they thought, "and she will cry out in disappointment!"

But gay on the air, rang a sound of gladness.

"See! Oh, see! My shoe is full!"

Astonished, Father and Mother hurried into the room. There stood Piccola with shining face, caressing her shoe, and cozily resting in it, lay—a bright-eyed little bird.

"It fell down the chimney and into her shoe!" her father said; but Piccola did not heed him. The bird had come as her Christmas gift, she knew. And every wish of her heart was satisfied and fulfilled. All day long she warmed the bird, and cuddled it, and fed it, till at last her father and mother, seeing how happy she was, caught her joy and were happy, too. So Christmas came to Piccola rich and full, because Christmas was always in her heart.*

*Taken from *My Bookhouse*, edited by Olive Beauprè Miller, with the permission of the publishers, The Book House for Children.

THE STORY OF TINY TIM

Tiny Tim was a little English boy. With clear blue eyes and fair hair, his cheeks should have been as hard and rosy as October apples. But they weren't. They were as soft and pale as only a little crippled boy's cheeks can be, for Tiny Tim had never walked a step without his crutch. But you must not think of him as being unhappy. He was the bravest, most contented little fellow in Camden Town, which is a shabby suburb of London.

Tiny Tim's mother said he was an angel of goodness. His big brother Peter, and his big sister Martha, and the two littlest Cratchits said so too. And his father, Bob Cratchit, was so sure of it that he was afraid Tiny Tim would slip away to heaven some day, to live with the other angels.

The Cratchits were very poor, for Bob was paid only fifteen shillings a week by Old Scrooge, in whose cold dark counting-house he was employed as a clerk. But poverty could not keep such a cheerful affectionate family from having a Merry Christmas. Tiny Tim's pale little face was

shining with joy when his mother began to cut up the little goose that was far too small for such a large hungry family, and he beat the table with his spoon and cried "Hurrah." And when father Bob lifted a cracked cup of water and wished them all "A Merry Christmas, God bless us," Tiny Tim responded to the toast with his favorite prayer:

"God bless us, every one."

When their few friends had been toasted, and the young and the old, and the sick and poor of London, father Bob lifted the cup again, and wished a merry Christmas for Old Scrooge. Mother Cratchit cried out:

"It should be Christmas Day, I'm sure, if one is to drink to the health and happiness of such an odious, stingy, hard, unfeeling old man as Mr. Scrooge!"

Remembering that it was a day of peace and good will, they all drank the toast presently, but their hearts were not in it. Old Scrooge was the wicked ogre of that little family, and even the mention of his name cast a dark and joyless gloom on the merriest of Christmases.

Old Scrooge did not deserve anybody's good will. He was so mean that he had grudged the Christmas holiday to his clerk. "You pick my pocket of a day's wages every 25th of December," Old Scrooge had snarled, and went home to his lonely old house to have a mean miserly Christmas Eve all by himself. When he had shut out the peace and good will that annoyed him he crouched over a stingy fire to spend the evening.

Perhaps he fell asleep. Anyhow, he thought he saw three spirits—the Spirit of Christmas Past, as Old Scrooge had kept it; the Spirit of Christmas Present; and the Spirit of Christmas Yet to Come. They showed him all his meanness and the misery that he had caused others, and how he was bringing upon himself a neglected old age, a wretched death, and a forgotten grave.

He was led to other homes of love and joy; and then to the poor little crowded cottage in Camden Town to see the happy family of good faithful Bob Cratchit. He heard the toast to himself, and saw the sudden gloom which the mention of his name brought.

Poor Old Scrooge! Poor, mean, stingy, cross-grained, lonely, wretched Old Scrooge! He suddenly knew how bad and pitiable an old man he was, and he envied his poverty-stricken clerk Bob Cratchit. He envied him his cheerful loving family and his cheerful loving heart; and most of all he envied him his frail little crippled boy who with the bravest sunniest smile cried out in a sweet reedy little voice like a bird's:

"God bless us, every one!"

The Spirit of Christmas Yet to Come showed Old Scrooge a vacant stool in the corner and a little crutch without an owner; and he knew that unless there was help here that money could command—good doctors, better and more food, and greater comfort in the crowded cottage —poor cheerful little Tiny Tim must die.

The Spirit vanished just as Old Scrooge woke up in his cold and cheerless old home. A sparkling Christmas morning had dawned. The whole day of Christmas Present was before him, but he was so unused to Merry Christmases that he didn't know what to do with this one. He laughed and cried both at once.

"I'm as light as a feather. I'm as merry as a schoolboy. I'm as happy as an—as dear little Tiny Tim. Merry Christmas!" He flung a window wide and shouted: "Merry Christmas! A Happy New Year to all the world! Hallo, there! Hallo! Whoop!"

Old Scrooge wasn't in the least crazy, for he began at once to do kind and sensible things just like anybody else. He bought the big prize turkey in the market, and to make sure it would get there in time he sent it to Bob Cratchit's cottage in a cab. Then he put on his gayest waistcoat and a beaming smile, and went to his nephew's to dinner like a Christian gentleman.

Bob Cratchit was eighteen minutes late at the office the next morning! He started to explain to his scowling employer (who was trying to look as mean as ever and finding it hard work) that he had eaten too much of a prize turkey that had come out to Camden Town like a lord, when Old Scrooge gave his bewildered clerk a friendly dig in the ribs, raised his salary, and told him to put a whole scuttle-full of coal on the fire.

That very day, after Merry Christmas, he began to be a second father to Tiny Tim. The darling child simply *couldn't* die so long as there were good doctors, good food, and other comforts in the world, and Mr. Ebenezer Scrooge had a pocket full of money. And the next Christmas, when the little crippled boy was stronger and healthier, the happy Cratchits thought first of their dear good friend, Mr. Scrooge, when Tiny Tim responded to the toasts with his loving prayer: "God bless us, every one!"

THE SNOW MAN

One day we built a snow man;
　We made him out of snow.
You should have seen how fine he was—
　All white from top to toe!

107

We poured some water on him,
And froze him, legs and ears;
And when we went indoors to bed
I said he'd last two years.

But in the night a warmer kind
Of wind began to blow,
And winter cried and ran away,
And with it ran the snow.

And in the morning when we went
To bid our friend good day,
There wasn't any snow man there—
Everything had run away!*

*By W. W. Ellsworth from *Live Language Lessons*, First Book. Published by The University Publishing Co., Lincoln Nebraska.

108

JAMIE WATT AND HIS GRANDMOTHER'S
TEA KETTLE

Jamie Watt, a little Scotch boy, sat by the great open fireplace in his grandmother's kitchen. Above the rosy, glowing flames there hung an old-fashioned tea kettle.

Jamie had been whittling a piece of wood, and making a cart with wheels, but now he dropped his work in his lap. Something had happened to the tea kettle that had caught his eye, and he began to watch it closely, for he never let anything strange pass by, without finding out the reason for it. The water in the kettle had begun to boil and a white column of steam was puffing out from its spout. Pretty soon, S-s-s! S-s-s! Piff! Piff! Piff! the lid of the tea kettle began to

rattle.   S-s-s! S-s-s! Piff! Piff! Piff! something
lifted the lid right up in the air!

"O Grandma! Grandma!" cried the boy in
great excitement.   "What is there inside of your
tea kettle?"

Grandma was busy laying the table for supper.

"Nothing, Jamie! There's nothing in there but water," she answered.

S-s-s! S-s-s! Piff! Piff! Piff! Up popped the lid again.

The boy watched it, breathless with interest.

"But, Grandma, there must be something inside the kettle," he insisted. "See! Something keeps lifting the lid!"

"Ho, ho!" laughed his grandmother. "Perhaps it's a brownie or a pixie you're thinking is in the kettle! No, no! It's only the steam that does the lifting! You can see the little clouds of it puffing out all around the lid."

Now Jamie wasn't thinking at all that it was a brownie or a pixie that was in the kettle. But he was thinking that he wanted very much to know what this thing called steam was, that had so much strength and power. Carefully he leaned over and lifted the lid to look inside. Nothing at all could he see but boiling, bubbling water.

"Grandma," he asked, "where does the steam come from? How did it get into the kettle?"

Grandma was used to his questions; he was always wondering about things.

"Why, dearie," she answered, "steam always rises from water whenever water boils."

The boy stood studying the kettle for a little longer, then he sat down again and while he was thinking and thinking, he began absent-mindedly spinning the wheels on the little cart he was making. At last he burst out:

"Grandma, if the steam in that kettle is strong enough to lift the lid, why couldn't steam from a great deal more water lift much heavier things? Why—why couldn't it push wheels around?"

"Push wheels around!" Grandma did not even try to answer so absurd a question. Jamie had strange and idle dreams, she thought, and she wished he would spend his time thinking of something more useful than pushing wheels around with steam.

But Jamie never left off wondering about the steam just the same, nor was his wondering so idle and useless as his grandmother supposed.

"That steam has the strength of a giant," he used to say to himself. "If I could only find out how to make use of it, it would not only lift heavy weights, but it would make all kinds of machinery go, and do all sorts of work."

So Jamie went on studying and working as he grew to be a man. Many times he made experiments with steam engines and his engines failed to go, but he always learned something new from each failure. Other people thought him foolish and laughed at him.

"Ho, ho! Jamie Watt is going to harness up the clouds that puff out of his granny's tea kettle and make them do the work of a giant!" they would jeer. But in spite of all this, Jamie worked on year after year until at last he did indeed make what no one had thought he could

—a steam engine that was a success. That was the Scotch boy's great gift to the world.

It was Jamie's engine that made possible the engines that draw trains, push steam boats, turn machinery, and do all the hundred and one useful things that steam engines do to-day. Men had lived for thousands of years beside that great giant, Steam, and yet not one of them ever learned how to harness it and make its mighty power of service to man, till one small boy began to think, and to question how it lifted the lid of the old tea kettle in his grand-mother's kitchen.*

*Taken from *My Bookhouse*, edited by Olive Beauprè Miller, with the permission of the publishers, The Book House for Children.

114

THE LAMPLIGHTER

My tea is nearly ready and the sun has left
the sky;
It's time to take the window to see Leerie
going by;
For every night at teatime and before you take
your seat,
With lantern and with ladder he comes posting
up the street.

Now Tom would be a driver and Maria go to sea,

And my papa's a banker and as rich as he can be;

But I, when I am stronger and can choose what
I'm to do,

O Leerie, I'll go round at night and light the
lamps with you!

For we are very lucky, with a lamp before
the door,

And Leerie stops to light it as he lights so
many more;

And O! before you hurry by with ladder and
with light;

O Leerie, see a little child and nod to him
to-night!

ABRAHAM LINCOLN'S EDUCATION

Abraham Lincoln did not have to wait until summer time to have a vacation from school; instead he counted up the days until it was time to have school again, for in Indiana, so long ago, there were more vacation days than days at school. The boys and girls had to wait their turn in having a teacher, for the teacher traveled about from place to place on horseback and stopped only a few weeks at each settlement. Then he passed along to another place where there were other children anxious to learn reading, writing and a little arithmetic.

So Abe went to school only a few months in his whole life; but he made those few months count. He spent all the time he could spare from his work in reading and studying. He had no paper, so he used a shovel, a large wooden shovel, on which to work out his problems. When the whole shovel was covered over with numbers Abe shaved off the top layer of wood with his pocket-knife and made a fresh place to write more figures with a piece of charcoal he took from the open fire-place.

Abe was not so fond of "number work." He liked to read best. There were very, very few books in his father's cabin, so Abe borrowed all

he could from the neighbors who happened to have a book or two in their houses.

Once he heard that a neighbor, Mr. Crawford, who lived across the woods, had a big book telling all about the life of George Washington, first president of the United States. The more Abe heard about that fine book, the more eager he was to read it for himself. So, in his bare feet he went over rocks and stubble, to Mr. Crawford's house. Mr. Crawford was not very anxious to lend the book. He told Abe it was a very expensive book and he would not be able to get another one like it very easily. But after a long talk and after Abe had promised to be very, very careful to see that nothing happened to the book, Mr. Crawford said he might have it just over night. So Abe went off holding his precious book under his arm. He planned to finish it as he sat before the fire-place that night. Then, he said to himself, he would take it back to Mr. Crawford the first thing in the morning.

However something happened to it and Abe was a very sorry boy when he woke up in the morning.

But now he was happy with the book under his arm. He read bits of it as he hurried home. He read of the many battles in which Washington fought. He read about the cherry tree that Washington chopped down when he was a very little boy. By that time he had reached home and his father called him to help with the work. Abe could scarcely wait for "candle-lighting-time," but it finally came, and then Abe was reading once more about his hero, Washington.

The night wore on, the candle sputtered and sputtered in its holder, getting smaller and smaller. Still Abe read on. He was at a thrilling part now; he was reading of battles. Just then the very last tip of the candle burned out—— Abe was left in the blackness of the loft, far away from the noble Washington, asleep in his pile of dry leaves, in the loft of the log-cabin.

The house was very still. All the folks were
asleep, had been asleep for many hours. Abe
dared not go downstairs, down the steep pegs in
the wall, to put the book away in the bog box
below. He dared not waken the family.

He felt around in the darkness for a safe
place to put the book. The only place he could
find was a big chink between the logs in the
wall at the side of his bed. Ah, thought Abe,

the book will be handy. In the morning I can read before any one is up." Carefully he slipped the book in the hole. Just before going off to sleep, he ran his fingers gently over the back to make sure that it was safe. Then he drew his deer-skin blanket close around him and fell asleep. He was very tired for he had worked hard all day in the fields, earning money for his father.

Soon after the lad went off to sleep, it began to rain. All night the rain poured down. In the early morning, Abe was awakened, not by the bright morning sunlight, but instead by the steady beat of the rain splashing through the chinks of the roof on to the loft-floor. His first thought was the book! Too late! All night long the rain had beat into the hole between the logs where the book had been hidden. Now the book was a soaking, sodden mess. Mud-plaster streaked the pages. The back and cover were loose, the rain had melted the glue. Every

bit of color was washed off the cover. Ruined!
Abe sat very still, the ugly mass crumpled in
his big strong hands. He could not think what
to do. It did not seem possible that the beautiful book that he loved could be ruined so
soon. What could he say to Mr. Crawford,
whom he had promised such care of his book?
Again and again Abe looked over the book to
see if he could not repair the damage, but he

could not even think. For every part was dimmed. Only the name, "Weems's Life of Washington," stood out clear and unstained. No, the ruin was done. The book could not be mended. Abe thought how furious Mr. Crawford would be. He remembered how careful this neighbor was of his possessions, and he had said the book was very, very valuable.

It would be a hard task to tell Mr. Crawford about his book, but immediately after he had brought in the wood for the breakfast fire, Abe went over to explain to his neighbor, and to say that he would mend matters in any way that Mr. Crawford would suggest.

"Well," said Mr. Crawford, "seeing that you are really so very sorry, Abe, and seeing it is you, I won't be hard on you. Come over and shuck corn for three days and the book is yours."

Thus Abe earned the book he loved so well. The book which might inspire any boy to dreams of being master of the White House.

THE RESCUE OF OLD GLORY

When Mother was making plans for a "safe and sane Fourth," Uncle Henry said, "Why not take the children to the park and have a kite party? I'll help them make the kites."

The next morning Harry and Anna were busy out on the porch with Uncle Henry. By ten o'clock three handsome white kites were drying in a row. Anna called them the "Big Bear, the Middle-sized Bear, and the Baby Bear."

When the kites were dry, the whole family started for the park—Uncle Henry with the Big Bear and a box of luncheon, Harry with the Middle-sized Bear, and Anna, of course, with the Baby Bear. Mother carried some sewing and Grandmother carried the surprise, something that

125

Uncle Henry had brought home in a flat box. When they reached the park, they found a French society holding a picnic. A tent was up, the band was playing, the older boys were shooting at a target, and the little boys and girls were flying red and blue balloons.

Uncle Henry said, "Ladies first, always," and he soon had the Baby Bear in the air, and the string in Anna's hands. He drove the bobbin into the ground, to make sure that the kite would not get away. Harry insisted upon putting his kite up alone. Then Uncle Henry put up the Big Bear, and when it was up some distance, he asked Grandmother to open the box. Then he shook out a red-white-and-blue silk American flag, and the crowd cheered.

Uncle Henry tied the flag to a loop of string, and fastened it to the Big Bear's string. Then he let it out, hand over hand. Up, up, went Old Glory, and snapped in the breeze. The

higher it went, the farther out the kite soared,
until it hung over the harbor.

They were all so busy watching it that they
had not seen that the picnic people below were
pointing up to the flag. When the band struck

up the Star Spangled Banner, every one began to sing. Then Uncle Henry noticed a boy who sang with a strange accent and great energy. The boy, whose name was Caspar, kept his big, solemn eyes on the flag that glowed against the sky. When he saw the others looking at him, he ran down the hill and hid behind the children.

"Any one who can sing the Star Spangled Banner like that boy is a good American," said Uncle Henry, as he drove his bobbin into the ground and prepared to open the box of luncheon.

When the French people went in to dinner, Caspar did not follow. He took his sandwiches, frosted cake, and ice-cream, and sat down on the grass, where he could look at the flag.

There was not a child in the whole park who loved the Stars and Stripes better than Caspar did, not even the two American children. In his own country Caspar had heard all about America, and how the Stars and Stripes were protected by even the poorest of little children. He had been told that our flag must never be harmed or trampled upon. After he came to America, his teacher had taught him to salute the flag.

He had heard the flag song on the big ship, and he felt that it was Old Glory that had brought him safe to one of his own country-women in America, with whom he lived.

Caspar was thinking of all this as he lay on the grass, and saw the flag fluttering in the light wind. He had watched it for some time, when he saw it give a quick little shiver, then begin to sink slowly, and then faster. He looked to the end of the line, and saw that the great white kite was dipping about in a strange man-ner; then he looked up to the hill and saw the kite man leaping down the hill as fast as he could. The American children were running be-hind him.

Caspar trembled with excitement. What would happen to the flag? Would it get trampled upon, or would it go out to sea and get wet and spoiled? Oh, he must help them get Old Glory! He ran until he was directly beneath the flag; then he stretched his arms high to catch it if it fell. But a strong breeze came up, and carried the Big Bear over the water, and pulled the flag with it. Caspar ran on to the water's edge.

Caspar did not know what to do next. There were no people on the shore, and no boats were near. The flag had not been trampled on, but it might fall in the water any minute. Where were the people? Didn't they know that something terrible was about to happen, to everybody in the park, to everybody in America, perhaps to the kind ladies who had been so good to him? How could the people sit about, eating and drinking, when there was such trouble in the world? He cried out to Uncle Henry and the children, who were now quite near, strange and broken words, and he tried to tell them that he could not swim.

"Good boy, swim for it! You'll get it!" shouted Uncle Henry.

Caspar understood the word "swim," but not the rest. He thought the kite man must be telling him that he could not swim, either. He looked out to the flag: it was surely going into the water; it flapped and dipped, then dipped deeper still, right into the water. Caspar did not wait another minute. Off went his jacket, and with a wild look toward the shore, he ran into the water. His feet slipped on the sandy bottom, and the kite jerked up, then down, then up—but it was always just out of reach.

They watched the boy, who was trying hard to keep the flag in sight. "Hurry, hurry, Uncle Henry, he can't swim a stroke!" shouted Harry.

Uncle Henry was just in time; Caspar had a firm hold on Old Glory and came up tangled in its folds.

After Uncle Henry had shaken the water out of the boy, he sat him on his shoulder, where everybody could see him. "Now, one, two, three!" he said, as he waved his free arm. "All

cheer for the boy who would not let the flag be
lost even if he couldn't swim! Hoo-ray!"

"Hoo-ray! hoo-ray! hoo-ray!" they said; and
then they cheered all over again, and crowded
round Uncle Henry and Caspar until the pair
started home to put on dry clothes.

When little Caspar went home that night, he
carried the flag that he had saved. Grandmother
had washed and dried it, and it looked as good
as new.

THE FLAG GOES BY

Hats off!
Along the street there comes
A blare of bugles, a ruffle of drums,
A flash of color beneath the sky.
Hats off!
The flag is passing by!

Hats off!
Along the street there comes
A blare of bugles, a ruffle of drums,
And loyal hearts are beating high:
Hats off!
The flag is passing by!

ST. CHRISTOPHER

Many years ago there lived in a land far across the sea a huge giant. He was very proud of his great strength and declared he would serve no one but the most powerful king in the world.

One day he set out to find this great king. Wandering about from one country to another, he at last came to one whose king was richer and braver than any he had met. The giant decided to stay here and glad indeed was the king to have so strong a man for his servant.

All went well until one day the minstrel who was singing mentioned the name of Satan. Offero noticed that each time he did so the king trembled and made the sign of the cross. Now, Offero had never heard of Satan and he did not know what the sign of the cross meant.

"Why do you tremble and why do you make that sign?" he asked.

"I am afraid of Satan because he is evil. I make the sign of the cross to protect me from him," the king answered.

"Ah! He must be greater than you if you fear him," exclaimed Offero. "I will go seek him."

Leaving the good king, the giant again journeyed through the land and after many days he met a mighty prince at the head of a great army.

"Who are you that so many men follow you?" inquired Offero.

"I am Satan," answered the powerful leader.

"Then I will serve you, for I seek for my

master the greatest king on earth," said Offero.

This greatly pleased Satan. "Come with me," he urged; "my service is not hard and I will give you pleasure and great wealth. Those who once follow me find it hard to leave me."

So Offero joined the army and went trudging on. One day, as they marched along a broad highway, they came to a large cross. Satan was startled and stopped suddenly.

"Why do you stop?" asked the giant.

Satan grew pale.

"You are trembling, too," said Offero.

"Yes, yes! I cannot bear the sight of the cross. I fear Christ Who died upon it. He is my greatest enemy," whispered the Evil One.

"You fear Christ. Then He is stronger than you and He shall be my King. I will go in search of Him at once."

Saying this, Offero left Satan. Many days he traveled and, weary and footsore, he came to the cave of a hermit.

"Can you tell me where I can find Christ?" he asked.

"That I can," said the pious hermit, "for He is the Master Whom I love and serve."

Bidding the giant sit down, the holy man brought him food and drink. After this, he related the story of our Lord's life.

Offero's heart was warmed with love for this new Master, but he feared he should be of little use to Him.

"I have nothing but my great strength to offer, and of what use would that be?"

"You must fast and pray," said the hermit.

"Oh," said Offero, "if I fast I shall no longer be strong and I do not know how to pray."

"Then," said the hermit, "I will tell you what to do. Do you see yonder rushing stream?

You must live by it and carry on your strong shoulders all who wish to cross to the other side. Let this be your work, and if you do it in God's name, He will be well pleased."

"That I can do and that will I gladly do," said the strong man.

So straightway he built a hut close to the river and, using a stout staff to lean upon, he saved many from the angry waters.

One night as he slept, a terrible storm raged. The wind blew and the thunder rolled. Suddenly, above the roar of the storm, he heard some one calling. The voice was low and fearful like that of a child.

"Carry me across, dear Offero," it cried. "Come and help me."

Offero arose and went out. At first he could see nothing, but, as the lightning flashed, he saw on the other bank a little boy, who held out his hands and cried to be carried across.

Without waiting to wonder why so small a child should be out in this wild storm, the giant plunged into the river.

As he reached the other side, the lightning flashed again. There stood the boy, close to the edge of the water. His thin clothes were soaked with the rain and he shivered from the cold.

"Do not be afraid, little one," said Offero. "We shall be across in no time and you will find shelter in my hut. Put your arms around my neck. Hold on tight; don't be afraid of hurting me."

The boy climbed upon the strong man's shoulder. He was so light that Offero scarcely knew he was there.

Offero turned and went down into the stream once more. The storm raged harder than ever and the waters rose to his waist. Never before did he have to fight so hard to keep from falling.

The weight of the child that was as nothing at first, became so great that he could scarcely stand. It was only after a breathless struggle that he reached the bank and placed the child gently on the grass. Then he looked at the child, around whom a strange light seemed to play, and said:

"Who art thou, little one? Often have I carried heavy burdens, but to-night I felt as though I had the whole world upon my shoulders."

"I am Jesus," said the Child. "In carrying Me, you not only carried the whole world but Him Who made the world and through Whom it was saved."

The strong giant fell upon his knees. He dared not raise his eyes.

"Lord," said he, "may I be Thy servant?"

"You shall be my friend," answered Jesus, "and your new name shall be Christopher; for

you have carried Christ on your shoulder. From now on, you shall carry Him in your heart."

Thus it was that St. Christopher earned his name. The old name of Offero, which means "The Bearer" has long been forgotten, but that of Christopher, or Christ-Bearer, will be remembered always.

HOW THE CHILDREN SAVED THE TOWN

Far up on one of the mountains of Italy
stood the little town of Spinalunza.

It was a lovely place, to be sure, for its houses
were neat and well kept, and a pretty white
church crowned the highest spot. About the
church was a grassy square, where happy

145

children played throughout the long summer days and where neighbors met in the evenings to rest and chat under the orange trees that grew all about.

Now, the mountain on which this town was built had three very steep sides which overlooked a deep ravine. Very few men had ever been able to climb up these cliffs. On the fourth side was built a high, broad stone wall. The heavy gates in this wall were well guarded, night and day.

The people who lived in this town thought it was the finest spot in the world, not only because it was a pretty place, but also because an enemy could attack it from only one side. For these same reasons the people of Pisa thought Spinalunza was a fine place too. Many times they had talked of attacking and taking the town.

One morning in early autumn, a stern captain

at the head of a large army of men and horses,
knocked at the gates.

"What do you want?" asked the guard.

"I am from the city of Pisa and I wish to
enter," replied the captain.

"That you cannot do," said the guard, and
he immediately rang a large bell which called
all the townsmen together.

When the men heard what had happened, they were very much disturbed. One of their number climbed into a high tower over the gates and called down to the captain from Pisa.

"Why have you come to Spinalunza? What do you want?"

"The soldiers from the city of Florence are attacking us and we are afraid you may help them if they ask you to. All we ask is a pledge that you will not join them against us. If you do not do as we say, we will burn and destroy your town," the captain answered.

"What pledge do you want?" demanded the man in the tower.

"We ask that twenty of your children ride back with us to Pisa. We promise that no harm will come to them and that they will be well cared for," was the answer.

The men inside the gates talked together. They knew they must think of a way to outwit this enemy, but how was it to be done? At last one man said:

"Tell him that to-morrow we will open the gates and all the children will come out. From them he may choose twenty."

That night the soldiers outside the gates spent their time in merry-making. Inside, while the children slept peacefully and unafraid, the mothers and fathers begged God and His Blessed Mother to help them find a way to save their children and the town.

Never before had such a terrible thing happened to Spinalunza. As the women prayed, they wept. Soon after midnight the fathers met in the churchyard to plan how to drive away the enemy. At last in despair, they decided to climb down the steep mountain side.

All through the darkness they climbed, crawling from bush to tree and tree to bush. Sometimes it seemed as if there were nothing but bare walls to cling to. Their hands were scratched and their clothing torn, but they did not mind that. As they struggled along, they prayed that God would see them safely to the valley below.

When they at last reached the bottom of the mountain, they divided into two bands. One band turned to the right and the other turned to the left. You see, they wanted to surround the soldiers who were waiting at the gates.

Morning seemed to come all too soon. When the sun was high in the sky, the church bell began to ring, the gates were opened and out marched the singing children, each child bearing on high a cross. The mothers stood and gazed after them.

Suddenly a strange thing happened. Every one was startled. The women rushed forward to find whether or not they were seeing aright. Behind each child walked an angel carrying a fiery spear.

As soon as the soldiers who had approached
the wall saw the great gates swing open, they
fell back in great fright. Panic filled their ranks.
Men who had been brave in battle trembled.
Horses plunged and threw their riders. All was

confusion. Men and horses fled alike in terror.

The men of Spinalunza had just reached the woods at the foot of the hill in time to hear the rushing army come tumbling down the slope. They could not imagine what had happened. They did not wait to inquire, however, but rushed out upon their enemy. The fleeing soldiers of Pisa went faster than ever, never stopping until they reached their own city gates.

All this happened many years ago, but the people of Spinalunza still tell the story of "How the Children Saved the Town." If ever you visit there, no doubt you will hear it too. Besides, you will see, standing in the square, the figure of a little child holding a cross and, close behind, that of an angel carrying a fiery spear.

THE WIND, A HELPER

The Wind Takes Janie to the Country

A little girl was once standing in a dark, narrow street playing with some bits of colored paper she had found. Suddenly a gust of wind came around the street-corner. It blew the colored scraps right out of the child's hand and carried them up over her head, then higher still, over the house-tops, until they were out of sight.

Janie, that was the little girl's name, watched them fly away, with tears in her eyes. Her busy mother had given her this day for a holiday, she had no toys to play with, and she loved those gay bits of paper. As she looked after the scraps up into the little patch of blue sky, which was all she could see between the high houses, she saw a small, white cloud scudding along, just the way the papers had flown.

"What makes the cloud fly so fast?" thought Janie, and as if in answer another gust of wind came blowing down the street. "Oh, wind, blow me, too," cried Janie, "take me up in the sky with the cloud," and she held out her little skirt.

The wind filled it and blew her—well, it didn't quite blow her into the sky, but it did a kinder thing. It blew her down the dark, narrow street, through other streets, each getting wider and cleaner, until at last it blew her right into the country. There she found herself racing over green fields, with the sky overhead so big and so blue that the clouds seemed like a flock of little sheep. There for a moment the wind left her— he had other things to do—and Janie stood looking around her happy and surprised. It was a spring day and the grass, which was waving in the wind, was soft and green and full of buttercups and daisies. "Far prettier than my scraps of paper," thought Janie. The trees were covered with new, green leaves, some of them were dressed in pink and white blossoms, and their branches swayed in the wind as if they were waving a welcome to the little girl. But she didn't have long to stand and look. Back came the wind, bringing new scents of blossoms and other sweet spring things with him, and off the child ran again.

Presently she saw in front of her a shining blue line, and when she reached it she found it was the sea. If any one of us has ever seen the sea on a clear windy day we can never forget it, and

that is just the way Janie felt. The waves were
high and blue, but they wore great white caps
which broke against the wind, and he scattered
them into foamy bits of spray, while the waves
came dashing over the beach.

Janie Learns About the Wind's Work

It was all so beautiful that Janie took a long,
deep breath of wind, and suddenly her cheeks
grew pink and her eyes bright, and you never
would have known she was the pale, sad little
Janie who stood in the dark street watching her
scraps of paper blow away.

She was standing on the beach gazing out to
sea in astonishment. For there, on the blue
water, was something that looked like a great
bird with its wings outspread, only it was far
bigger than any bird, and as it skimmed over
the water she saw men moving upon it. Can
you guess what it was? It was a splendid ship;
but as Janie had never seen one before, except

in pictures, she was much puzzled. "What
makes it fly so fast?" she wondered, and for an
answer the wind blew her along the beach,
through a garden, and almost into a little white
cottage, where a woman was standing with a
baby in her arms.

She didn't seem to mind a bit when she saw
a strange little girl come flying down the garden
path to her house. She just laughed and cried,

"This is another trick of my friend the wind." Then she laid the baby down in a cradle and took both of Janie's hands, making her sit on the door step where the wind had dropped her.

"Please, ma'am," said Janie, when she could get her breath, "can you tell me what makes the boat sail?"

The woman laughed again and answered, "Why, this beautiful wind blows her along, of course; that is only one of the hundreds of things the wind does for us. He can blow so hard that the great ships are just driven before him, and he can blow so softly that my baby is rocked to sleep. Look at the cradle now." Janie looked, and there in the light wind which seemed to be full of the scent of blossoms, the cradle was rocking so gently that the baby had fallen asleep. Then the mother brought Janie a bowl of bread and milk, and while she ate it they talked about the wind.

"He blows away the dead leaves with such

fury," said the mother, "that they tear along in front of my window like a flock of frightened birds. But when he finds a little flower beneath the leaves he blows on its petals so softly that it feels as if its mother were kissing it.

"Sometimes, when it comes from the North, it brings snow and hail and the beautiful frosts of winter. But when it comes from the South it brings sweet scents and soft, warm air. The East Wind often brings rain and mist, and some people don't like it, but the ground needs the rain, the flowers love it, and the East Wind is a gift from God, just as the others are. The West Wind is blowing to-day, and that is why the world looks so fresh and shining."

So they talked most of the afternoon, the mother and Janie, until the sun began to sink and when the ship came sailing homeward, Janie turned again towards the city.

Very gently this time the wind blew her along, beside orchards where the trees were rustling their leaves like lullabies, and through meadows where, like sleepy children, the flowers were nodding their heads for good-night to the dear West Wind.

JANIE RETURNS TO THE CITY

And although she was leaving it all, Janie was very happy. The woman in the cottage by the sea had told her to come back on her next holiday. And she knew that although she could not always see the dancing trees and flowers and waves and ships, she could remember that they were waiting for her every time she heard the wind rattling the window and blowing among the chimneys.

Just before she went to sleep she looked out of her window through which a patch of sky could be seen. It was a dark cloudy patch, and Janie was just turning away from it when the clouds began to move. The wind was still at work. In an instant the clouds had been

blown away, and through that window Janie saw a bright, clear star shining down upon her.

"Thank you, dear wind," she whispered. And then, as she cuddled down to sleep she seemed to hear the wind, or was it the star, singing softly, "Thank God, thank God."

THE WIND

I saw you toss the kites on high
And blow the birds about the sky;
And all around I heard you pass,
Like ladies' skirts across the grass—
 O wind, a-blowing all day long,
 O wind, that sings so loud a song!

I saw the different things you did,
But always you yourself you hid.
I felt you push, I heard you call,
I could not see yourself at all—
 O wind, a-blowing all day long,
 O wind, that sings so loud a song!

O you that are so strong and cold,
O blower, are you young or old?
Are you a beast of field or tree,
Or just a stronger child than me?
 O wind, a-blowing all day long,
 O wind, that sings so loud a song!

THE SILVER BELT

DAH-CHEE LEARNS TO SHOOT

Dah-chee was a little Navajo Indian boy, who lived far out in the west.

The big desert was his home, and not far from where he lived was a wonderful canyon.

Little Dah-chee was never allowed to enter this canyon alone, for there were snakes

163

to be found on the warm sandy bed in summer, and in winter the rains made big patches of quicksand that were not safe to walk upon.

But Dah-chee liked this big canyon best of all play places. He loved the big dark walls, and the eagles' nests high up in the cliffs, and the places to climb and hunt for little animal trails.

Sometimes his father would take him into this wonderful place, and he loved these little journeys, as his father always pointed out so many interesting things.

Most of the Navajo men wore beautiful belts, made of bright silver disks strung on a leather thong, and none were more beautiful than the one worn by Dah-chee's father. Always he had wanted one, too. He thought if he had one for his very own—well, he would be the happiest Indian boy in the world.

When he became eight years old, his grand-father brought him a new bow and a lot of bright red arrows. My, but Dah-chee was happy! He had never owned a real bow before, and he danced up and down for joy. Out he ran into the desert and began to look for something to shoot at. A big cottonwood tree stood close by, and on the side of it, his grandfather tacked a piece of sheepskin. It shone white against the dark wood and made a good target. Then he set a large stone on the ground, about twenty feet from the tree, to mark the place where Dah-chee was to stand when shooting.

"To-morrow," said his grandfather, "I go back to my home in the desert. In seven days I will come again to see you. If, when I come, you can shoot well enough to hit the sheepskin mark once, out of five shots, I will give you a silver belt. If you do not hit the mark, the belt will not be given to you. Only Indian boys who

shoot well should wear the belt that warriors wear."

Then the old man went away, and each day little Dah-chee tried very hard to hit the mark. At first he couldn't even hit the tree. The arrows simply wouldn't go where, he was sure, he was aiming them. Then one day he found that he could hit the tree every time, and at last, on the day before his grandfather was to come again, he was able to hit the piece of sheepskin twice out of five shots.

That day was a long one for Dah-chee, and he felt that the morrow would never come. He not only wanted the long-wished-for belt, but he was going to show his grandfather how well he had learned to shoot. He was very sure he would have no trouble hitting the mark, at least once with five arrows.

Again and again he thought of how wonderful the new belt would look about his waist. Wouldn't he be proud of it?

When the long expected day came, he was up before the sun, testing the string of his bow, to make sure that it was just right.

As soon as it was light enough to see, he began shooting at the mark, and he kept on shooting until his arms ached and his little legs were weary with running after the arrows.

It was late in the morning when his grandfather rode up to the hogan, which is just the Indian name for home. With him was a white man, a lady, and their little daughter. The little girl looked to be about Dah-chee's own age. Parties of white people often came to visit the wonderful canyon, in the summer time, and as they were almost always guided by his grandfather, Dah-chee was used to seeing them stop at his home.

On this particular morning it seemed an age before his grandfather had finished attending to the white man's horses, and had the many camping things packed, for the party was to start up the canyon later in the day, after the lady and little girl had rested. But at last the old man came to Dah-chee, and seeing he held five arrows and the bow in his hand, he said,

168

"Well, Dah-chee, we will now see how well you can shoot."

They went over to the big cottonwood tree, and taking his stand by the stone, Dah-chee quickly shot the first of the five arrows. It missed not only the sheepskin mark, but the tree as well. It may be that he was a little too excited or too anxious; anyway he had four arrows left, and only one was needed to hit the mark. His grandfather said nothing, but waited for him to shoot again. The second arrow hit the tree, but struck the bark some distance from the sheepskin. At last, when four of the five arrows had been used, the old man spoke kindly to his little grandson.

"I believe you have saved the last arrow just to show me how easily you can hit the mark. Though you now have but one arrow, it is as good as ten, if it hits the sheepskin."

At his grandfather's words, Dah-chee grew

more calm, and his arms were more steady as he raised the bow for the final shot—the shot that *must* hit the mark, if he was to get the belt. Just as he was taking careful aim, he heard the little girl and her father coming. Anxious to shoot before they came up, he let the arrow fly a little too quickly, and it struck the tree far below the bit of sheepskin.

His grandfather walked away without saying a word, for he was a wise old man, and knew that his promise to his little grandson must be kept. The little boy hung his head, and turned away without stopping to pick up his arrows. Then, fearing that the little white girl might follow him, he ran as fast as he could to some great rocks that stood far out in the desert. Dropping behind one of the rocks, he lay with his face to the sand and cried as though his heart would break. It didn't seem real, or true, that he *could* have missed the mark each time, out of the five shots.

He had lain there a long time when he suddenly heard the sound of footsteps near at hand, and a moment later his father stood beside him. He did not seem to notice the tears that still stood in Dah-chee's eyes, as he said,

"Your grandfather is ready to take the white people into the canyon, and he says that, if you wish to, you can go with them."

Dah-chee was on his feet in an instant, and soon had forgotten the great disappointment of the morning as he rode along in the wagon, pointing out the many interesting things to the little white girl.

Later in the afternoon, when they had ridden a long way, his grandfather told them all to get out of the wagon, and to walk a while to stretch their legs. All were glad to obey, and jumped out on the smooth white sand.

The high canyon walls cast big cool shadows, which were welcome, as the day was very warm. Dah-chee's grandfather drove the wagon slowly, and behind it, in single file, came the white lady, then her husband, and the little girl, with Dah-chee the last in the line. This just suited him as he had his bow in hand, with an arrow on the string, ready to shoot at any bird or animal that might be careless enough to show itself.

Soon he and the little girl were some distance behind the others of the party, each gazing delightedly about them at the many things to be seen.

"Oh, look at the lovely red rocks over there by the canyon wall!" cried the little girl. Then she called to her father, "Look, Father! What a fine place for a play house! Let's all go over and see it." And she pointed towards the place as she ran.

Without waiting for her father, who had turned back when he heard her call, she ran on to the pile of rocks, followed by Dah-chee who was some little distance behind her. She reached the spot, and stopped short as she heard a queer, dry rattling noise that was not like any sound she had ever heard before.

As she turned to see what could be making the sound, she saw, so near to her that she could have touched it, a great rattlesnake coiling itself on the flat top of a rock. For some reason she found she was unable to move. Her father, who had heard the noise of the snake, ran forward as fast as he could, and cried out with fear as he realized that he was too far away to reach his little daughter before the snake might strike her.

Then above the dry rattle of the snake was heard a far different sound; it was the twang of Dah-chee's bowstring, and a second later the

big snake was twisting harmlessly on the rock
with a red arrow through its body.

Then the white man acted very foolishly; at
least Dah-chee thought he did, for as soon as
he had caught up his little girl, and realized
she had been saved, he picked up Dah-chee also,
and hugged him close, while tears of joy ran down
his face.

Surely, thought Dah-chee, no Indian man
would ever do a foolish thing like that.

When the little boy's grandfather and the little girl's mother had heard the white man's cry of alarm, they came running up to learn the cause. The white man and the little girl told them all about the big snake, and of how Dah-chee had made the wonderful shot, just in time to save the little girl from being bitten. Dah-chee did not care for the praise of white people— what could *they* know about good shooting? —but his grandfather, well, if *he* was pleased, that was a different matter, for he knew all about such things.

The old man, who had said nothing, reached into a large leather bag, that was suspended from his shoulder by a thong, and drew out a package. From this he produced a beautiful new belt whose bright silver disks shone in the sun like polished mirrors. And still without a word, he knelt beside Dah-chee and fastened it about his waist. Then he rose and said,

"Dah-chee, you have given proof that you are worthy to have the silver belt, and I believe you will some day be a good guide and a good warrior."

But Dah-chee scarcely heard his grandfather's words, though they were words of greatest praise, for his little hands were wandering over the smooth silver disks of the beautiful belt, and it was really *his*, his very own.

ST. DOROTHY, GOD-GIVEN

The iron gate slammed, and Dorothy was alone. Down the white road strode the senator's son, his toga flying in the wind.

For the first time in her life the little maid was afraid. Her face was as white as the snowflakes now whirling about her. She drew her cloak closer with a little shiver, not wholly from the cold.

Her eyes followed the fast disappearing figure of the angry boy. She had refused to marry him because she had promised herself to Jesus Christ, and all her sweet, pure love was given to the Heart of God. Theophilus would tell the Emperor that she was a Christian, then would come terrible tortures and death. Oh, would she be brave enough to suffer then, when now she was trembling at the mere thought of the flames and sword? Tears came to her eyes. She was only a weak girl, and the soldiers were so strong.

Then a thought quieted her. The name, Dorothy, meant "Gift of God." Her life was the dear Lord's gift. If she offered it back to Him bravely for His sake, would He not be with her even in the midst of the flames, to give her strength and courage?

Her lips smiled, her arms fell apart. "Dear God, I am not afraid now," she whispered, her face upturned to the gray skies.

A few months later a crowd without a prison waited for a sight of the girl martyr. Because she would not bow before the idols, Dorothy had that very day been condemned to death. As they watched, the gates swung wide, and Dorothy, her wrists bound, and guards on either side, came forth. Her step was firm, her sweet lips smiling, but her eyes modestly cast down.

Theophilus was among the watching throng. As she passed him, he cried mockingly, "You are going to die for God, you say. I will believe that there is a God if you send me roses and apples from His garden."

Dorothy raised her eyes for a fleeting instant, then dropped them again. "I will send them," she answered simply.

That night, while Theophilus was trying to
drown the memory of Dorothy's death in a gay
banquet, a little child stood suddenly by his
side.

On one arm was a basket of crimson roses,
and nestled deep down in the dark green leaves
were apples, too fair to have been grown
in the gardens of earth. "Dorothy bade me
give these to you," a sweet voice whispered.

Theophilus turned, startled, but the boy had disappeared. Only the basket with its fragrant burden of fruit and flowers remained.

"Here, catch that boy," he cried to the servants. "What boy?" they asked. "We have seen no one."

Theophilus waited not to answer, but sped out into the night. White-faced, he sought the city streets. Glaring lamps flashed at intervals along the dark ways, and by their light he peered wildly into hidden places. But no sign of the little one. Terror lent wings to his feet. Men turned to look after him, but he cared not. Dorothy's face, pure and sweet, gleamed before him, and urged him on. If the wee messenger were an angel of God, and the roses had come from His eternal home, then the faith for which the martyr had died was true.

All the long night he searched in vain, and the still hours of dawn found him prostrate in the open fields outside of the city gates. He pressed his hot face to the cool, green grass, and the first prayer of his life sprang to his lips.

"O God of Dorothy, have mercy on me," he sobbed. "I believe, I believe."

One by one he remembered the words she had spoken to him, their sweetness and earnestness, and above all, her generous forgiveness, when she knew he had sought her life. Ah, the God whom she loved so dearly must be the true God.

A few brief months, and his new-born faith was strangely tested. As Dorothy had done, he stood before the great tribunal, thrilled by the thought that she had listened to her sentence, perhaps, on that very spot. Bravely he confessed Christ, and won the martyr s crown. The prayers of the girl martyr had been answered in Heaven.

A SPRING LILT

Through the silver mist
  Of the blossom-spray
Trill the orioles: list
  To their joyous lay!

"What in all the world
  In all the world," they say,
"Is half so sweet, so sweet,
  Is half so sweet as May?"

"June! June! June!"
  Low croon
The brown bees in the clover.
  "Sweet! sweet! sweet!"
    Repeat
The robins, nestled over.

FAIRIES

The wee folk are about, dears,
    For near the oak you'll spy
The toadstool tents, their mimic camp,
    Amid the grasses high.

And on each bush this morning,
  Still damp with misty suds,
Were gauzy cobwebs stretched to dry,
  Their little fairy duds.

All in the moonlit midnight,
  While folk a-sleeping lay,
The elfin court held carnival
  And danced till break of day.

I saw the firefly lanterns
  And heard the throb and hum
Of the cricket fiddlers' tuning shrill
  And the June bug's low bass drum.

And where they held their revels
  And danced beneath the moon,
Were shining dewdrops on the sward,
  The print of fairy shoon.

SAN MIN'S TREASURE

Perhaps you think it would be great fun to have a boat for a house. San Min, a little Chinese boy, had lived in just such a house. Not once in the ten years of his life had he ever been away from it—not even for a day. He spent much of his time fishing and watching the seabirds fly over the marshes.

San's father was a fisherman and many times a week he took the fresh fish and eggs to the market. When he returned, he told wonderful tales of the city, with its beautiful temples and gay shops. How San wished that he too could see these wondrous things! This wish, to see the things he thought of by day and dreamed of by night, was soon to be granted. One fine morning his father said to him:

"Come, get up and dress quickly, for I am going to town to-day and you may come with me."

The little lad jumped up and scrambled into his clothes. At last he was going to see the country beyond the river! He was so excited that he scarcely touched his bowl of rice.

It took but a short time to reach the city, and the never-to-be-forgotten day began. It was a festival day—the Feast of Lanterns. The narrow streets were brilliant with lovely colored hangings. Gay lanterns, strung in every possible way, swayed back and forth in the gentle breeze. San thought the children who lived on the house-boats and the wild birds who flew

screaming over the water made noise enough,
but here everybody was talking at once and
everybody was in every other body's way. It
was all so new and wonderful to the little river-
boy that his bright brown eyes danced and shone
with excitement. More than once he rubbed
them to see if he were awake or dreaming.

As he trudged along, gazing all about him and
wondering where all the bright and beautiful
things had come from, San noticed two sweet-
faced, white-robed women, wearing black veils
that hung down their backs. They smiled at his

questioning little face, and when they passed, he turned to look after them. As he did so he noticed that they had dropped something. Because all Chinese children are honest and polite, San ran to pick it up. What he found was a little black cross with the figure of a man on it. This interested him so much, that for a few moments he forgot the Sisters—for of course, good Sisters they were. It was only when he heard his father calling him that he remembered what he had intended to do. He looked everywhere, but the women were nowhere to be seen. They were lost in the crowd.

San felt sorry that he had not run after them at once. He knew that there was nothing for him to do now but keep the cross and hope that some day, when his father took him to the city again, he would be able to return it to its owners.

The rest of the day passed all too quickly for San. After it was dark and the lanterns had been lighted, his father said they must start for home. When they reached there, it was a very tired and sleepy boy who tried to tell his mother all that had happened during the day.

Although for three years San did not again leave his river-home, he never forgot the wonderful day that he had spent in the city. As he fished or worked about the house-boat, he often thought of the crucifix and would take it out and look at it. As he looked he thought:

"Who is this Man? Why is He nailed to the cross? How hard it must have been to have died that way."

If only he could find the woman who had dropped it. Maybe she would tell him all about it.

There were many other house-boats on the river besides the one in which the Mins lived. There were hundreds of them and they were so close together in some places that they bumped against one another.

When San was thirteen years old, a terrible thing happened. Crowds of people were taken sick and died. Those on the crowded houseboats did not escape. Many of them died too, among them San's mother and father.

The little fellow was very sad. His only comfort seemed to come from the cross which he always carried in his pocket. Whenever he looked at it, he felt glad that his parents had died at home and had not been nailed to a cross. He thought he never could have stood that.

Now that he was alone, San tried to be very brave and to carry on the work that his father had done.

One day he started for the city with his fish and eggs. How surprised he was when, instead of the bright lanterns and gay flags that he had seen on his first visit, he now saw closed windows and quiet streets. The boy could not imagine where all the happiness had gone. He did not

know that sickness and death had been here
too.

Just as he was about to return to his river-
home, for he thought it was brighter there than
in this dark place, he saw, coming towards him,
the two white-robed figures that he remembered
so well.

He had the cross with him. "Now," thought
he, "I can give it back."

Running as fast as he could, he overtook the
Sisters. Breathlessly he told the story of how

he had found the cross and how he had kept it until he could return it to its owners.

When the Sisters heard San's story, they looked at each other in surprise. The cross which this Chinese boy held in his hand belonged to one of them—Sister Claire.

"Will you please tell me who this Man is and why He is nailed to the cross?" San asked.

The Sisters wished to talk with the boy but, as they had much work to do, they could not stop there on the street. San was delighted when they asked him to walk along with them. He not only walked with them, but went everywhere they went that day. At one house they cared for a poor woman; at another they baptized a little baby. As San watched them, he thought how much happiness and comfort they brought wherever they went.

When the Sisters had done all they could for that day, they started towards home. It was not until then that San asked them:

"Why did you not come to the house-boats on the river to help my mother and father and the other people who were ill?"

Sister Claire smiled sadly as she answered in a tired voice:

"Little San, we should have come gladly, but there are only six of us in this crowded city. Sometimes, in times like these, our hearts are sad because we can do so little for the souls we have come to save."

San didn't understand what this meant and asked:

"Why aren't there more of you? Can't you get some others? They can have my boat for a house!"

"There are many, many more who could come and would if they knew how much we need them. We will ask our God, 'the Man on the Cross,' to send them," said Sister Claire.

By this time the Sisters had reached their home, an orphanage where many children were cared

for. Sister Claire asked San to come in and sit
down for a few minutes to rest and talk. Now
she told him the story of the Cross, and as she
did so, tears rolled down his cheeks.

Think of it! Tears from this heathen boy for

Christ on the Cross, and you and I who know Him so well and can visit Him so often in our churches and take Him into our hearts, hardly give Him a thought, much less a tear!

After Sister Claire had finished telling the story, she gave the cross to San. How proud he was to think it was his very own. That night he slept with it tightly clasped in his hand.

Many times after this, the boy visited the orphanage. The kind Sisters taught him his prayers, the very same ones that you and I learned when we were very little. At last, one day, he was baptized and received our Lord in Holy Communion. He never could tell how very happy he was on this day.

San grew to be a kind, good man who loved God with all his heart. He told the Story of the Cross to many of his people, and they also learned to know and love our Lord. Because of this, the Sisters always called him, their "Little Apostle, San of the Cross."

THE HERO OF HAARLEM

Along one of the canals in the old Dutch city of Haarlem, there lived many years ago a little boy named Hans. One day his mother called him from his play.

"Come! Hans, come!" she said. "Take these cakes to the old blind man who lives on the other side of the dike. If you hurry, you will have time to go and return before it is dark."

Hans was very happy as he trudged along whistling a merry tune and swinging his basket on his arm. His wooden shoes went clatter, clatter over the rough stone pavements.

Little Hans' visit made the old blind man very happy, and the boy stayed to talk much longer than he had intended. The two talked of many things, but Hans liked best to hear tales of the sea and of the brave men who had built the great walls to keep it from coming in over their land. "For you know," the old man would remind him, "Holland lies much lower than the ocean."

When Hans started for home once more, the sun was setting. He knew that he must hurry, for supper would be ready and his mother would be waiting. Besides, had he not told his little brother and his sister that he would be home long before the first star was in the sky.

"I'll run along the top of the dike," he thought, "for that is the shortest way."

As he ran, he watched the angry waters dash against the wall.

"You are wicked, Sea," he said aloud, "and would like to spoil our fields and houses. Well for us that our gates are strong and my father tends them carefully or they would not hold you out long."

Just then he saw some beautiful flowers growing in the meadow. "Mother would like those,"

he thought, and down he ran to pick them. When he was about to climb up the bank again, he saw a few drops of water trickling through the wall.

"It is a leak in the dike! A leak in the dike!" he exclaimed. At once he remembered all that his father had told him of the cruel strength of the sea and how the water coming in through a tiny opening would quickly wash away the dirt and stones of which the dike was built.

The boy grew pale with terror. He looked

all about for something with which to mend the hole, but there was nothing to be found. Then, quick as a flash, he squeezed his fingers into the place, and was relieved to find that it held back the water.

Now he shouted for help. Again and again he called, but the place was lonely and no one came in answer to his calls.

It was not long before the sun set and the night grew darker and darker.

Hans was afraid, for the only other time that he had been away from home at night was when he had stayed with the blind man. The cold wind made him shiver. Sharp pains ran up and down his arm. His finger hurt but still he held it there bravely. He thought of his father and mother, of his little sister and brother. They were asleep in their safe, warm beds and no harm would come to them if he could prevent it.

No; no matter how his arm and shoulder

ached he would not forsake his post. God would give him the strength and courage he needed; this he knew.

All through the night the waves beat against the wall. As they beat, they seemed to say:

"Give way, little boy, give way! Who are you to dare stand in my path? Do you not know that I am the great sea?"

Hans tried to be brave, but it was a struggle to keep back the hot tears. "Dear God," he prayed, "please help me to keep the water from coming in over our land."

Once more his heart was filled with courage, and he shouted:

"No matter what you say, Old Sea, you can't drive me away. God will not let you destroy our fields and our houses."

Poor Hans was so stiff from lying on the cold ground all night that when morning came he could scarcely move. At last, when the sun was well up in the sky, he heard the sound of footsteps. Tramp, tramp, they came, nearer and nearer. Soon he saw two men coming towards him.

"Help! Help!" he cried.

The men stopped suddenly.

"Who calls for help? Where are you?" one of them shouted.

"I am here," answered Hans, "at the foot of the wall."

The men rushed down the bank.

"Why, it's Hans, the gate-keeper's son," said one of them whose name was Jan. "Come, lad, what are you doing here? Why, you are blue with the cold!"

"I could not leave. There is a hole in the dike and I am keeping back the water," replied Hans.

Gently Jan raised the child to his feet. In a moment he saw that all the boy said was true. The tiny stream again began to trickle and gurgle.

It did not take long for the two strong men to mend the dike. Every man in Holland knew how to do that. When the work was finished, they placed the boy on their shoulders and started back to town. They called to all they met to tell them of the boy's brave deed. Of course, a great crowd began to follow them.

When the men reached the little cottage where Hans lived, Jan called to the father and mother,

"Give thanks, for your son has saved our land and God has saved his life."

At first the poor parents could not understand what had happened. They thought the boy had spent the night with their old friend, the blind man, and now they were surprised to see him sitting on the shoulders of these strong men.

The mother and father were proud and happy indeed, when they heard the story of their son's bravery. As the mother clasped him to her heart, the crowd cheered and shouted, "Hurrah for Hans, the boy who saved Haarlem!"

All this happened many years ago, but the Dutch people still tell their children the story of Hans' brave deed. When they speak of him they call him the "Little Hero of Haarlem" and they say he is the boy whose prayer God answered when he asked for strength and courage to save the city from the sea.

THE LITTLE TOY LAND OF THE DUTCH

Away, 'way off 'cross the seas and such
Lies the little flat land of the Dutch, Dutch,
    Dutch!

Where the green toy meadows stretch off to the
    sea,
With a little canal where a fence ought to be!

Where the windmills' arms go round, round,
  round,
And sing to the cows with a creaky sound.

Where storks live up in the chimney top,
And wooden shoes pound, plop, plop, plop!

Where little toy houses stand in a row,
And dog carts clattering past them go!

Where milk cans shine in the shiniest way,
And the housemaids scrub, scrub, scrub all
  day.

Where dikes keep out the raging sea,
And shut in the land as cozy as can be.

Oh, that little toy land, I like it much,
That prim little, trim little, land of the Dutch!*

*Taken from *My Bookhouse*, edited by Olive Beaupré Miller, with the permission of the publishers, The Book House for Children.

THE SILVER BELL

I. The Silver Bell Is Placed in the Tower

In a country far across the sea there was long, long ago a very old church. It was so old that no one knew when it had been built. In the tower of the church there hung a large silver bell.

Now there was something strange about this bell. No one had ever heard it ring, nor was there any living person who could truly tell how it had come to be placed there.

In the town where the church stood, there lived an old man. He liked to tell the story of the silver bell as his father had told it to him when he was a little boy. This is what he said.

Many years ago a kind prince lived in the big gray stone castle that is close to the top of the hill. He was loved by every one and was known far and wide for his many deeds of kindness. The prince loved the people of the land as dearly as they loved him, but he was often troubled because he found as he went among them that they were not always happy. One day, when he was standing in the church square watching all that was going on about him, the thought came to him, "These people are unhappy because they have grown selfish. They no longer love their neighbors as themselves, and are not kind to the poor and needy. Something must be done to remind them of their selfishness."

At last he thought of a plan by which to help them. He ordered his servants to hang a great silver bell in the tower of the church. When it was in place, he said to the people:

"The notes of this bell are said to be the sweetest in the world. The bell, however, must not be rung until a person has been found who truly loves his fellow-men. If at the end of thirty-three years no such one has been found, it must forever remain silent."

Years passed and the thirty-three years were almost at an end. Still the bell gave forth no sound. Finally the people began to wonder whether or not they should ever hear the sweet music for which they had listened so long.

It was at this time that great troubles came to the land. During the summer there had been but little rain and, as the crops did not grow, the fathers had little money with which to meet their needs throughout the winter. Worse than all else, many of the people were taken sick and no one seemed to know what to do to help them. It was indeed a time of sadness.

II. THE KING WHO LOVED HIS FELLOW-MEN

Now, the king of this country was a very young prince who had just come to the throne. In the palace there had always been many servants to wait upon him and he had always had everything he wanted. Scarcely ever had he seen any one who was poor or in trouble.

It was not strange, then, that the people said, "This king is young and has never been taught to share the troubles of others. He can know nothing of our needs."

The young king, however, had a kind and tender heart even though the people did not think so. At night when every one was sleeping he would kneel and pray for the sick and the poor. Then he would dress himself as a peasant and would steal out of the palace, carrying large bundles of food and clothing.

Up and down the dark and silent streets he would go, leaving his treasures at the homes of the needy ones. He worked thus, night after night, from evening until daybreak, until he became so ill and worn that he could scarcely stand.

His gifts of food and clothing helped make the hearts of the people happy once more. Very soon the fathers and mothers began to say to each other, "Surely this poor man who is help-ing us is unselfish. Who can he be?" One neighbor asked the other, but no one knew. At last one of the fathers said, "Come, we will go to the palace and ask the king. Perhaps he may know who this man is or he may help us find him."

Away they hastened. They told the young ruler all about the gifts they had received and the poor man who had brought them.

"Can you tell us who this man is or will you help us find him?" they asked.

"Be contented, my good friends," the king replied. "Is it not enough that God has sent His servant to you in your time of need?"

This answer did not please the people. They turned, one to the other, and said, "The king does not know how we have suffered, so he cannot know how grateful we are. He has been sitting in the palace eating good food and

212

wearing fine warm clothes while we have been cold and hungry in our poor homes.

"Since he will not help us find the man who has been so kind to us, let us ask him to let the silver bell be rung for him," said one of the men.

Once more the king listened to what the people had to ask. Then he answered, "That I cannot do. Only God can tell whether or not any one is worthy of so great an honor. Go and pray to Him and ask that He send an angel from on high if there is one among you who truly loves his neighbor as himself."

III. THE SILVER BELL IS RUNG

That evening the people went to the church and many of them stayed all through the night to pray. In the morning, when they were leaving to return to their homes, a strange thing happened.

213

A bright light broke through the clouds and
shone upon the church tower. Then, lo! the
silver bell began to ring.

The men and women were astonished. They
knew that no living hand touched the bell. The
music was the sweetest they had ever heard.

It sounded as though hosts of angels were singing. They knew that God had answered their prayer.

As the crowd stood there listening and watching, the bright light faded. In its place there appeared the words, "It is your king who truly loves his fellow-men."

A look of shame crept over the faces of the people. This was the man against whom they had murmured.

They fell to their knees and asked God to forgive them.

Once more they hurried to the palace—this time to thank the king who had been so kind to them and to try to right the wrong they had done. When they reached there they found they were too late. The palace gates were closed. The angel who had rung the bell had entered before them and had taken away with him the soul of the king who had tried to bring much love and kindness into the world.

RIDDLES

Come, let you in a circle sit,
And use your tongue, and show your wit,
In guessing riddles, who can beat,
The one who does, deserves a treat.
Perhaps you know some riddles old,
Some ones that are but seldom told;
If you do, pray tell them here,
For riddles always bring good cheer.

GUESS ME

OR

IF YOU CAN'T,

HOLD ME TO A LOOKING-GLASS

I saw a host with a million blades,
  A million blades or more,
Upon a hill or in the lane,
  And at the cottage door.

"Alas!" I cried. "Against such host
   Who will my good lands keep?"
But when I had thought twice, I sent
   An army of my sheep.

(GRASS.)

'Tis not to be bought for silver or gold,
The more you put in it, the more it will hold.

(THE MIND.)

What king with banners bright
Can eat a city in a night;
But who, though such a greedy sinner,
Will humbly cook a peasant's dinner?

(FIRE.)

What giant with lofty brow hath but one foot?

(A MOUNTAIN.)

What runs without feet?

(A BROOK.)

217

Neither lord nor lady I, but always bear a title;
Neither tree nor bough nor bush, but always
  have I leaves.
However much you take from me, I lose nothing.

(A BOOK.)

Riddle ree, riddle right,
Stays at home, day and night.
Yet wanders far
To sun and star,
Follows bird on wing
Or rests on cloud or creeping thing.

(THE EYE.)

Although they live in the selfsame place,
One seldom sees the other's face.
When he's abroad, she hides away
He goes—she comes in bright array.

(SUN AND MOON.)

218

THE CALICO'S STORY

Once I was very tiny and all covered over with a brown coat. I had many brothers and sisters; we lived in the sunny South, and were kept huddled close together in a strong bag.

One morning the people who lived in the house were up earlier than usual, and I heard the master say: "Tom, you may plant that cotton seed to-day." Cotton seed was my name, and I wondered whether it was better to be planted than tied up in a bag. But while I was thinking, Tom picked me up with the others, and I was soon put into a little bed close to a rolling river.

I loved to listen to the water as it laughed on its journey to the sea. I wanted to see it, but

my coat fitted so closely that there was no
chance.

I began to feel larger, and larger, until one day
my snug coat split, and I popped right out of
the ground. Wasn't I happy then? I had a
green body and two green leaves. I stretched
my head higher and higher, and at last I had
three beautiful blossoms. I think I must have
been vain, for all my beautiful petals left me,
to go with Mr. Wind. I mourned for them
every day, but, to my surprise the little bolls

left by the blossom burst, and I was covered with cotton as white as snow and as soft as silk!

I was as happy as a queen! The cool wind fanned me, the sunbeams came to warm me and the dear old river lulled me to rest. Then one day the master and a lady came riding past. The master stopped for a while and looked all about. I heard him say, "I must tell Tom to pick the cotton to-morrow."

The next morning very early, Tom came with a dozen other men. When one of them saw me he cried out, "Oh, did you ever see finer cotton?" In an instant I was held in his fingers. Next I was riding in a basket on top of Tom's head; then in a cart on my way to the "gin." I was sorry as I left the fields, and said: "Good-by, old body and leaves. Good-by, dear river."

When I got to the "gin," a machine took from my downy grasp many little fellows dressed in brown coats. They looked just as I did before I went to sleep in Mother Earth.

My next trip was in a bale. I was loaded on a big ship which sailed on a great sea. I liked this bale and the ride. It made me think of the river where I used to live.

By and by the ship stopped.

I was carried to a large house where I heard "buzz, buzz, buzz." So many strange things happened to me that I wondered what would be the end of it all. I was cleansed and twisted

222

and spun and woven and bleached, and at last found that I had become white cloth.

My next journey was through a printing machine. At first I was white, but this machine sent me under a roller which left little bunches of red cherries all over me. Then I went under another roller which put green stems on the cherries and left green leaves close to the stems. A third roller left brown twigs where all the leaves and stems ought to hang. Prettier bunches of fruit you never saw.

Now my white was almost gone, but what was left was made black by a fourth roller.

I went under these rollers so quickly—a mile an hour—that I could not see very much, but I know that cherries were cut into the first roller, and that they had red dye on them; the leaves and stems were cut into the second roller and covered with green dye; the twigs were cut into the third with brown dye all over them.

I wondered if some of the leaves, twigs and stems might not print themselves in the wrong place, but they never did.

After I left the black-dye roller, I was dried, folded and sent to a shop in a noisy city, where I lay on a shelf.

One day a little country girl came into the store with a basket of eggs. She wanted to look at me and, just think, she gave the shop-keeper all of her eggs for eight yards of me.

Then I was made up into a dress, with pretty ruffles at the neck and sleeves, and I gave much joy to the little girl, who always liked to wear dainty things.

On her way to and from school, she used to sit upon a log to rest. Here I used to watch the plants which grew near, but they were very unlike my old self because they did not grow in a warm country. What I enjoyed most of all was a river which flowed near and sang the same song as my old friend.

THE DUEL

The gingham dog and the calico cat
Side by side on the table sat;
'Twas half-past twelve, and (what do you think!)
Nor one nor the other had slept a wink!
  The old Dutch clock and the Chinese plate
  Appeared to know as sure as fate
There was going to be a terrible spat.
  (*I wasn't there; I simply state*
  What was told to me by the Chinese plate!)

226

The gingham dog went "Bow-wow-wow!"
And the calico cat replied "Me-ow!"
The air was littered, an hour or so,
With bits of gingham and calico.
  While the old Dutch clock in the chimney-place
  Up with its hands before its face,
For it always dreaded a family row!
  (*Now mind; I'm only telling you*
  What the old Dutch clock declares is true!)

The Chinese plate looked very blue,
And wailed, "O dear! what shall I do!"
But the gingham dog and the calico cat
Wallowed this way and tumbled that,
    Employing every tooth and claw
    In the awfullest way you ever saw—
And, oh! how the gingham and calico flew!
    (*Don't fancy I exaggerate—*
    I got my news from the Chinese plate!)

Next morning, where the two had sat
They found no trace of dog or cat;
And some folks think unto this day
That burglars stole that pair away!
    But the truth about the cat and pup
    Is this: they ate each other up!
Now what do you really think of that!
    (*The old Dutch clock it told me so,*
    And that is how I came to know.)

HOW PRIMROSE WENT TO THE PARTY

The Prince who lived in the great white castle at the top of the green hill was to give a party, and he had invited the children from the village to come.

For days there had been talk of little else at the cottage doorsteps, and in the market place. Oh, the children all knew how wonderful a party at the Prince's castle would be. The doors would be thrown wide open; in all the rooms there would be rose trees of every kind and color; birds would sing in golden cages; and each child would be given a feast and precious gifts.

There was something else, though, that the children knew. One must be dressed in a fitting way to appear at the castle of the Prince. Each child knew that he or she must appear in the best that they had to wear.

Well, that was easily arranged. They nearly all had ribbons, and there were bits of fine lace laid away in the home chests that could trim their frocks. Pieces of velvet were to be had and the village tailor was busy, night and day, making ruffled shirts and fine suits for the boys, while the mothers stitched and embroidered for the girls.

But when their party clothes were made, another thought came to the children. They should, themselves, carry gifts to the Prince.

This, also, was arranged. A bit of old carving from this cottage, an old silver cup from that shelf, a basket of rare fruits from this fertile orchard. These were good gifts.

So, at last, the children started up the hill to the castle. All were ready to meet the Prince, they felt sure, except Primrose; she walked apart from the others, for she had no party dress and no gift to carry.

She was named Primrose because she made a

poor, bare little hut on the edge of the forest bright, just as a wild flower makes a waste spot beautiful. In all her life Primrose had never been to a party, and now she was invited with the others. But her feet were bare, and her little brown dress was torn, and she had no hat to cover her wind-blown, yellow hair.

As they went up the hill, the children passed a poor fagot gatherer, bending under her great bundle.

"Off a pleasuring, with little thought for
others," the old woman mumbled to herself, but
Primrose stole up to her side and slipped one
soft little hand in the woman's hard, care-worn
one.

"I will carry half your fagots for you to the
turn of the road," she said. And she did, with
the old woman's blessing on her sunny head
at the turn.

Farther on, the children passed a young thrush that had fallen out of its nest and was crying beside the road. The mother bird cried, too. It was as if she said,

"You have no thought of my trouble."

But Primrose lifted the bird in her two hands and scrambled through the bushes until she had found its nest and put it safely in. The branches tore her dress that had been ragged before, but the mother thrush sang like a flute to have her little one back.

Just outside the castle gates, there was a blind boy seated, asking alms.

When the other children passed him, laughing and chattering of all that they saw, tears fell down the cheeks of the little blind boy, for he had not been able to see for a long, long time.

The others did not notice him, but Primrose stopped beside him and put her hands softly on his eyes.

Then she picked a wild rose that grew beside the road and put it close to his face. He could feel its soft petals, and smell its perfume, and it made him smile.

Then Primrose hurried through the castle gates and up to the doors. They were about to be closed. The children had crowded in.

"There is no one else to come," the children shouted.

Then they added, "There is no other child except Primrose, and she has no dress for a party and no gift for you, great Prince."

But the Prince, his kind eyes looking beyond them, and his arms outstretched, asked,

"What child, then, do I see coming in so wonderful a dress and carrying a precious gift in her hand?"

The children turned to look. They saw a little girl who wore a crown; it was the fagot bearer's blessing that had set it upon her head.

Her dress was of wonderful gold lace; each
rag had been turned to gold when she helped
the little lost bird. In her hand she carried a
clear white jewel, her gift for the Prince; it was
a tear she had taken from the little blind
boy's face.

"Why, that is Primrose," the children told
the Prince.

THE ELF AND THE DORMOUSE

Under a toadstool
Crept a wee Elf,
Out of the rain
To shelter himself.

Under the toadstool,
Sound asleep,
Sat a big dormouse
All in a heap.

Trembled the wee Elf,
Frightened, and yet
Fearing to fly away,
Lest he get wet.

To the next shelter—
Maybe a mile
Sudden the wee Elf
Smiled a wee smile;

Tugged till the toadstool
Toppled in two.
Holding it over him,
Gayly he flew.

Soon he was safe home,
Dry as could be.
Soon woke the dormouse—
"Good gracious me!

"Where is my toadstool?"
Loud he lamented,
And this is how umbrellas
First were invented.

LATE

My father brought somebody up,
    To show us all, asleep.
They came as softly up the stairs
    As you could creep.

They whispered in the doorway there,
    And looked at us awhile.
I had my eyes shut up; but I
    Could feel him smile.

I shut my eyes up close, and lay
    As still as I could keep;
Because I knew he wanted us
    To be asleep.

ST. TARCISIUS

Long ago there lived in the city of Rome an orphan boy named Tarcisius. In those days the Christians were obliged to hide for fear of being put to death. If they were caught, they were cast into prison and tortured. Those who were willing to give up their faith and become pagans were set free. The others were loaded with chains and placed in dark cells to await some form of cruel death.   They are known as martyrs.

The Christians had no churches.   Instead they dug deep tunnels under the ground in which they gathered at certain times to receive the Sacraments and hear Mass.   These dark passages, called catacombs, were lighted only by candles, and were entered by secret openings placed far outside the city, and known only to the Christians themselves.

Tarcisius, though very young, often went to the catacombs with the other Christians.   While there he used to hear about the prisoners who were soon to die for their faith.

How these holy martyrs longed to receive our Lord before they went forth to die!   They needed the Blessed Sacrament to give them strength to be brave.   But the danger of sending It to them was very great.   The priests did not dare to go themselves, for they were well known to the pagans, and if they were caught they would be put to death. But worse than this, the Sacred Hosts would be shamefully treated. Some holy man, therefore, was usually chosen for this important work.

Tarcisius hoped that some day he might be allowed to bring our Lord to the prisoners, but because he was so young he did not dare to ask for this great favor. Our Lord, however, Who loves to dwell in the hearts of little ones, soon granted his prayer.

One day before Mass the priest, turning to the people, asked, "Is there any one here ready to face death? Our brethren in the prisons have sent word that they are waiting for Holy Communion. But our enemies are on the watch. Pray during Mass that God's will may be made known."

Saying this, the good priest offered his Mass. When he had finished, the tiny form of Tarcisius approached the altar. "Father," he whispered, "if you will let me carry the Blessed Sacrament, the pagans will never guess."

Tenderly the priest gazed on the earnest face of the child. "You are so young, my boy," he answered.

"But, Father," pleaded the lad, "I am not afraid. Do let me try. Just because I am little, they will never know what I carry."

The priest was silent for a moment, but his eyes were moist.

Then placing his hand on the curly head, he faltered, "You shall have your wish, my boy, and may God protect you!"

Wrapping the Sacred Hosts in a pure white cloth he placed them under the tunic of the happy boy, and with a fervent "God bless you," he told him to be off in haste, lest the Christians should be put to death before he arrived.

Tarcisius, carrying the Blessed Sacrament and with his hands clasped over his heart, hurried away on his great errand.

Over and over again he kept saying to
himself, "My Jesus, I love You! My Jesus,
I love You!"

As the Little Messenger sped along, looking
neither to left nor to right, he was startled by
some one calling his name. "Tarcisius! Tarcisius! Why do you hurry so? Come and play
with us!" insisted several childish voices at
once.

"Not to-day," he answered gently, with a glance at his tunic, "I have important work to do."

"What is that you are holding under your tunic?" demanded one of the roughest of the boys.

Instead of answering the question, Tarcisius whispered a prayer. "My Jesus, help me!" he murmured.

At this, his youthful playmates bore down upon him to find out what he carried. One, wiser than the rest, cried out, "He is a Christian! He calls upon their God to help him!"

At the word "Christian" they began to abuse him. Some struck him; others hurled stones at the frail little form. Tarcisius tried to run away, but he was helpless against so many. At last, weak from the blows he had received, but still clinging to his hidden Treasure, the faithful Little Messenger fell to the ground.

Just then a soldier happened to be passing by. Seeing what had taken place, he cried out in anger, "Begone, you cowards!" and soon scattered the young bandits.

Then raising the dying child in his strong arms, he said tenderly, "Such a little lad to lose his life for Christ!"

At this, Tarcisius opened his eyes and looked at the soldier. "You understand," he gasped, "for you are a Christian. I have seen you in

the catacombs!" Then pointing to the spot
under his tunic where the Sacred Hosts still
rested, he pleaded, "Take Him the rest of the
way for me; they are waiting for Him." Then
the little head fell back, and the brave little heart
ceased to beat.

"Noble child!" exclaimed the soldier, "I will
finish your task; and who knows—maybe I,
too, shall follow!"

A CHILD'S WISH

I wish I were the little key
    That locks Love's Captive in,
And lets Him out to go and free
    A sinful heart from sin.

I wish I were the little bell
    That tinkles for the Host,
When God comes down each day to dwell
    With hearts He loves the most.

I wish I were the chalice fair,
    That holds the Blood of Love,
When every flash lights holy prayer
    Upon its way above.

I wish I were the little flower
  So near the Host's sweet face,
Or like the light that half an hour
  Burned on the shrine of grace.

I wish I were the altar where,
  As on His Mother's breast,
Christ nestles, like a child, fore'er
  In Eucharistic rest.

But, oh! my God, I wish the most
  That my poor heart may be
A home all holy for each Host
  That comes in love to me.